ASTROLO
PALMISTI
and
DREAMS

CW00433671

ASTROLOGY
PALMISTRY
and
DREAMS

by

DONALD LAW

Ph.D., D.B.M., Dip.D., Psy.D.,
D.Litt., M.N.T.A., phil.med.D.

JOHN BARTHOLOMEW & SON LTD
EDINBURGH

First published in Great Britain 1973
by John Bartholomew and Son Ltd
12 Duncan Street,
Edinburgh EH9 1TA
and at 216 High Street,
Bromley BR1 1PW

ISBN 0 85152 922 4

Printed in Great Britain by
Bristol Typesetting Co Ltd, Barton Manor, St. Philips,
Bristol

DEDICATION

To my friend Pekka Nuorala of Raahe
without whose help it would not have been written.
Kiitos ystävälleni Pekka Nuoralalle
työstään kirjan valmistelussa.

Contents

Chapter 1

Astrology, Key to Fate and Fortune

At a date remote in prehistory, Man detected some relationship between the planet Earth and constellations in space. Whenever certain groups of stars stood in specific places the rains came, the snows made the land silent and cold, the harvest came – always something seemed to happen.

It was not difficult to extend these observations until one compared the behaviour of other human beings to the relationship of the stars to the planet Earth. The fact that similar behaviour patterns were clearly observable led to oral and later written records being kept – the foundation of the science.

By careful deductions, sage observations, and keen eyes, men learned to steer their ships by the position of the stars. How simple to move from this to the adventurous logic of steering not only one's ship but also one's life by the same stars!

The word *Zodiac*, meaning the twelve signs through which Earth seems to pass, has been translated as the circle of animals, but this ignores the original Greek meaning of *Zoe* which is *Life*. Think of the Zodiac as representing the *Circle of Life* and its relevance is such that we are struck with the wisdom of those distant ancestors of the Human Race as we know it today.

There are indications in the book of Dr. Immanuel Velikovsky (*Worlds in Collision*, 1952) that originally the world may have taken only 360 days to make its ellipsoid movement around the Sun; hence the Babylonian, Assyrian, Egyptian and Ancient Chinese calendars of 360 days (12 months of 30 days each) were perfectly correct, and the old Maya calendar of 18 months, each of 20 days equally so. It is further possible that what we know today as a fringe science had its origins in some extraordinarily highly-developed knowledge dating before the flood (legends of which exist in the epic of Gilgamesh, the Bible, Norse and other mythologies). Then it may have been that men knew why the planet Jupiter was associated with prosperity, wealth and growth . . . and so on. Long ago in Ancient Egypt a Zodiac (found at Tevcros) showed 36 signs, each of which governed 10° only – but still the 360 days are predominant! The speculative will be tempted to ask whether these signs were the navigational aids of voyagers in spacecraft of another age? Indeed the older the literature the more there is indication of 18 constellations, and we know that it is a usual human tendency to simplify things: There is a suspicion that the individual human memory capacity is deteriorating. At the beginning of this century there were a few Somali Imams who could recite the entire Koran by heart, and quote accurately from it – chapter and verse; there are 6,000 verses! When Elias Lönnrot wandered the wilds of Karelia in the 1830's he found ancient Finns who knew the many thousands of verses of the *Kalevala* by heart, having learned them in a father-to-son tradition. Too late we realise that there are gaps in the ancient knowledge – like many of the ancient Hindu works on astrology.

It has long puzzled me that the Zodiac we use makes use of constellations which are quite difficult to identify but seems to ignore some like *Orion*, which was named in the East after the saviour-god Tammuz the beautiful who was slain for men's sins and rose again to restore life to the dead. ' *Canst thou bind the sweet influences of Pleiades or loose the bands of Orion?*' demands God of Job (Chapter 38, verse 31).

Another mystery of the Zodiac in almost any known form is the prevalence of certain ideas in widely separated parts of the globe – unless we begin to look at the possibilities of early, lost civilisations such as Atlantis and Mu. Figures such as Leo the lion, Aquarius, etc., figure in some recognisable form in almost all Zodiacs, regardless of the date.

There seem fairly reliable indications that the entire universe is revolving around the celestial polar regions.

The star we call *Draconis alpha* or *Thuban* was the polar star about 4,000 years ago, when the Great Pyramid of Cheops was constructed, and then each night the cold light of this master star shone down the entrance to the main chamber of the pyramid! What knowledge lies hidden! How little men know!

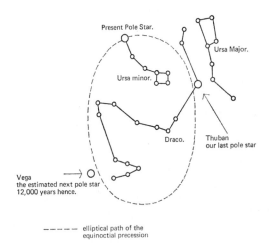

It has sometimes been objected that Astrology cannot have any relevance upon human life because *the times they are a'changing*, but there is a further detail here which some people have neglected – the speed of light! Travelling at the speed of light – 186,000 miles per second – one would have to travel for millions of years before one could carry the light and any other rays from a constellation to this planet, so recent (by our measurements) changes of the earth's position vis-a-vis the constellations are hardly relevant in themselves in view of the colossal time factor involved. This knowledge of the equinoctial precession was first recorded by Hipparchos (c. 190–125 B.C.) who also listed 1,022 stars, classified them according to size, brightness etc. – not bad for a man without a reflector telescope! At this stage let us try to understand what a star is. It will give us a better comprehension of radiations and power. It is a common fallacy that a star is a solid body, but modern astronomy and space research have shown that a star is a sphere of glowing gases, shining entirely by its own power, the pent-up pressure of which is at present entirely beyond human comprehension – and at temperatures quite inconceivable in human terms of measurement. Its combustion would seem to be similar to nuclear chain reaction, so the star is not consumed – as is coal for example.

To put this sort of thing into figures – our Earth weighs about 6,000,000,000,000,000,000,000 tons! The diameter of the Earth at the equator is 7,926 miles, the diameter of the Sun is approximately 860,000 miles! Its average distance from our planet is 93,000,000 miles. The galaxy of which we are a part is said to contain some 100,000 million stars such as the sun. From the broadening of the spectral lines the kinetic temperature of a star may be estimated – that of the Sun is about $5,800°$ K, but some stars rise to about $50,000°$ K. The energy behind such fabulous temperatures can scarcely be guessed at.*

Many of us were told in our physics lessons that a wave is a regular oscillation which spreads itself from an energy source through a medium such as space. Ripples on the surface of a pond show us how transverse waves move.

* Kelvin degrees, based on Absolute Zero at $-459°8°$ Fahrenheit or $-273°16°$ Centigrade.

The direction seems to be horizontal; small particles of energy or matter move up and down on (through) the surface substance of the medium, it is not the medium that moves but the disturbance.

In order that we can better appreciate the strength or volume of power behind these sources of energy I would add that whereas the speed of light gives us a measurement of one light year of about 5,880,000,000,000 miles, this measurement becomes too small for relevance and a *Parsec* equal to 19,150,000,000,000 miles is used as a basic unit to start counting.

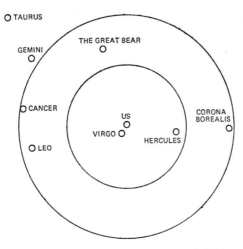

US : includes not just our earth and our solar system BUT also Andromeda 575,000 parsecs away from our planet. The entire Milky Way is also included!
The first, inner ring is at a distance of 5,880,000,000,000 x 200,000,000 miles away from Earth.
The outer ring is at a distance of 5,880,000,000,000 x 400,000,000 miles away from Earth.

All these measurements and theories assume that the physics laws of outer space are the same as those for our own solar system.

I will now offer some ideas as to how influences in the form of vibrations can travel across the *caverns measureless to Man.* There are in space electric and magnetic fields of activity which seem to act perpendicularly to one another and to the line of the propagation of electro-magnetic waves which, it is known, can radiate through even a vacuum!

If unhindered by solid matter the electro-magnetic radiations proceed at the same speed as Light, e.g. 186,000 miles per second (300,000 kilometres); evidence hitherto available indicates that these radiations can be refracted (bent) and even reflected from a surface without losing their power; moreover they seem to be capable of curving along a specific gravitational field without any appreciable loss of volume.

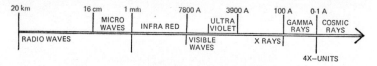

A.: Ångström unit of measuring light waves, named after Anders Jonas Ångström, Swedish physicist (1814—74).
1 A : A hundred million-th of a centimetre.

It will be clearly seen that the range of invisible radiations far exceeds the miniscule range of visible rays, and the range of cosmic rays is, at present, suspected rather than fully known.

Governments have set up expensive establishments to report upon the nature, purpose and functions of cosmic rays – without much worth-while return for their money. and *it may be*, that somewhere within this range of vibrations there are influences from the constellations, or the Zodiac as we say.

From interstellar space these extremely rapidly-moving rays penetrate the upper atmosphere of this planet. While it is known that low-energy rays come from the Sun, others of colossal energy emanate from sources classified by scientists as *unknown.* They come from all directions (12 zodiacal directions) and ionise the air we breathe. One is forced to consider the importance the ancient Hindu sages ascribed to the air and the way of breathing it in for the *development of the Mind*.

Those that enter the atmosphere are primary rays, and as such perhaps too strong for human beings. These rays strike atoms of oxygen and nitrogen some 10 miles above the earth, and from the collisions emanate secondary rays. *Primary rays have been measured by geiger counter*. Their known nuclei include light elements such as hydrogen or helium, but some with mysterious nuclei nearly 100 times lighter than the charge on a hydrogen atom have been recorded.

One thing is increasingly clear – there is order, harmony and mathematical precision throughout the entire range of Space, but it is of such an order and so highly developed that we can scarcely begin to guess at it. There is Bode's law (1772) showing the numerical relationship of the solar system planets – take 6, 12, 24, 48, 96, 192 and 384, each of which numbers is double that before it, add to each number four, and you have the scale of distance of Earth, Mars, Ceres (minor planet or asteroid), Jupiter, Saturn, Uranus, Neptune and Pluto from the Sun: Bode's law is not very exact for Mercury or Venus which lie between Earth and Sun, but only for the outer planets. Tycho Brahe (1573) who established on Hven Island (near Elsinore) the first really modern centre for studying the stars – a fact of which Danes are very proud – explained the elliptical motions of planets, something more difficult to observe than a simple circle, for an ellipse is basically a shape resembling an egg. It is still fashionable (because they are easier to draw) to show planets in circles around the sun, but it is impossible to show this of a comet.

A comet is a body which seems to be largely nebulous, revolving around the Sun in a flattish, drawn-out ellipse. As long ago as the 9th Century A.D. the Chinese astrologers noted that a comet's tail always points away from the Sun. Many comets seem to make their ellipsoid movement round the Sun touching the orbit of the Earth and the orbit of another planet, e.g. Jupiter. We may one day be in a position to investigate whether they bring some specific radiational influences from one orbit to another.

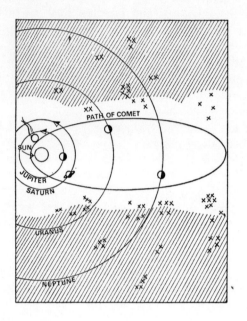

Another phenomenon which seems to be a visible sign of radiations coming to Earth is the extremely beautiful *Aurora Borealis* (there is also a southern counterpart called *Aurora Australis*).

These brilliantly coloured, dancing lights range from 40-200 miles in height above the earth. It is now thought that they are caused by currents of electrically-charged particles of solar energy streaming towards our atmosphere. It is conceivable that our planet is a magnet of some sort with the poles a true North and South (magnetically speaking) and it is significant that this energy radiates powerfully in the polar regions of the planet.

Only a detailed study of radiesthesia and the nature and

role of vibrations in the universe can explain the possibilities inherent in this type of solar activity.

The magnetic effects upon our planet also relate to the equinoxes and solstices, as our Earth revolves around the Sun to produce spring, summer, autumn and winter – a season for everything.

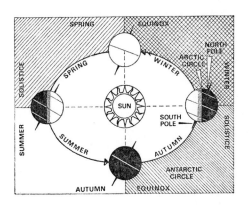

It is a far cry from the orderly, exact horary tables carved by Egyptians for their priesthood, whereby if a man sat in such and such a position on such and such a day he would see this star and that planet on his left shoulder, and others on his right.

So much we know – the Earth proceeds around the Sun; during its orbit certain constellations are visible and in specific places during the journey. People born within specific periods show generally recognisable traits of character and behaviour. Radiations come to this planet. They may be related to these characters and trends. My purpose in writing this work is to present the collected observations which apply more or less to the bulk of people born under each specific sign of the zodiac.

The Ancient Egyptian Zodiac had 36 signs, and it is probable that the Zodiac signs we now use are not wholly adequate to explain the variations within its limits. A person who is Aquarian born, but within one or two days of Pisces, will probably display one or two traits of Pisces rather than those of the central Aquarian period – and so on.

Each one of us reading a delineation of character will incline to admit some things (good or bad) and deny others; occasionally we may know instinctively that one is wrong, another is right; sometimes we may be so near to the portrait that the perspective of ourselves is at fault . . . or as Burns put it :– *wad some pow'r the giftie gie us to see oursels as others see us.*

One thing is remarkable : whoever named the Zodiac knew human nature very well, was extremely learned in patterns of animal behaviour and something of an artist to picture these forms in the tracings of the stars, and he must have been an exceptionally gifted astronomer to recognise them.

There is a tropical Zodiac, which is measured from the tropics, and which moves; there is a sidereal Zodiac which takes its measurement from fixed stars but in relationship to the calendar moves forward one day every 72 years! At some time shortly after the birth of Christ the two were more or less mathematically identical. When we speak of the tropical Zodiac we mean the four tropics or *turning-points of the Sun* (See illustration 5). It would seem that at such points there are strange things in space – incomprehensibly huge nebulae of gases with ultra-violet radiations, etc.

The movement of the planets through the signs of the Zodiac has long been accepted as a series of modifying influences. The Hindus claim that the positions of the Moon also affect horoscopes, and several western astrologers have accepted this.

It has been objected to astrology, by those who have only a shallow understanding of it, that over the last 2,000 years the position of constellations has changed. Such alterations as we perceive have taken many millions of light years to reach this planet – so can hardly be said to be *of recent date*. The influences affecting us may well have left their sources many millions of years before any such changes took place. Nor does this indicate predetermination, since at best these influences appear to be of the nature of *tendencies* rather than of dictates.

The great herbalist abbess, Hildegard von Bingen (1100–1179 A.D.) believed that the stars revealed much about the past, present, but nought of the future.

It is the prediction of the future that earns many astrologers their daily bread, to say nothing of a yacht on the Riviera.

Enormous publicity is given to successes, scant notice to the failures. Spectacular successes are recorded, but I think it is wise to realise one or two simple facts. *Roughly one twelfth part of the world's population is born under each sign.* The predictions appearing in a daily paper (e.g.: ' *You may speculate today – and nothing will go wrong* ') can hardly be accurate for hundreds of millions of people.

A highly specialised horoscope by an accredited expert will be of far more use, and is likely to achieve an accuracy which will satisfy, if not surprise, the recipient.

All predictions are based upon likelihoods and trends, behavioural patterns, character failures, weaknesses, virtues etc. which are commonly found under such a sign.

As old Baron Münchhausen said : *A man must know how to help himself*; to build one's entire life up upon predictions, to make no move without predictions, may in some circumstances make for a secure life, but never for an individual life : such a life enables us to blame others or our stars for our misfortunes more than we blame ourselves.

To a positively orientated person *difficulties are there to be overcome*. Astrology makes a useful guidepost but an unsatisfactory prop, and to pin one's entire hopes, life and prospects upon this or any other one method of prediction is likely to lead to disappointments : Many things in this world are excellent in moderation when intelligently used and applied – wine for example; it is a sign of maturity when a human being can learn the possibilities, weigh the probabilities and then act according to his or her own judgment.

The facts of astrology are clear for all who read; how astrology is used and how many are its uses is often debated. It is my earnest hope that this section of the book will contribute towards Man's appreciation and understanding of this great fund of knowledge.

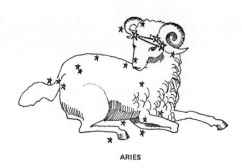

ARIES

Aries the Ram: (21 March to 20 April)

You are among the most energetic and dramatic people in the world. Given a goal you will force the pace, regardless of difficulties, to reach it. No sign is so resolute and tough in the face of opposition, resistance and hindrance. You tend to regard difficulties as coolly as a mathematical problem which can be solved if you give enough time to it. You may get knocked down but will bounce back up again with great resilience. You will rarely spare yourselves to get what you want, least of all other people. If you fight Aquarians you will lose – they are an air sign and it will be like punching a ball of smoke.

You tend to be headstrong, to rush at life head-down – it is inevitable that you will sometimes get hurt – until you learn to accept other people's rights and allow them their dues.

Will-power is not the only virtue in this world. Don't forget that *the top can be very lonely indeed.*

You often fail to foresee the consequences of your actions – and several acts of your life are the result of impulse, will-power and stubbornness.

You are adventurers, lovers of success and frequently suffer from dissatisfaction with people, places and your possessions. Many of you are cursed by restlessness.

Dreams and desires often supersede logic in your thinking – unfortunately the gap between dreams and reality is enormous.

Often Aries complain that friends desert them or that their lovers are untrue – the tragedy is in their own nature; they would be more popular if they used other people less for their own ends.

In spite of your charm, interesting – often witty – conversation you are at times far less concerned with your fellow human beings than they, in their innocence, believe.

You readily suspect enmity where there may be nothing more than mild disagreement. You like to make a pattern of clear black and white in a world full of different hues of grey.

You rarely appreciate how much your intensely positive approach to life can exhaust others. Outwardly you seem very friendly, sympathetic and are always entertaining and humorous: You seldom criticise yourself and do not much approve of criticism from other people.

Habits, good or bad, can master you. Beware of alcohol or drugs – for Aries subjects they are very dangerous. At worst Aries may degenerate to fanatics and professional rebels. Aries must strive for education for without it there are dangerous pitfalls that ruin the Aries, hold him back and frustrate him badly.

Aries are not extremely successful in the field of the arts, but their greatest successes seem to lie within literary and musical activities.

There is something that smacks of primitive man in the

Aries folk, you make the best soldiers, but you prefer in every aspect of life the simple frontal attack – you despise deviousness and complications, diplomacy, trickery and the like – nevertheless you can use such devices to attain your own ends.

Your temper is rash but you seldom hold a grudge. You are not good at keeping secrets, your own or another's.

The Aries woman can only truly love a man whose will is stronger than her own.

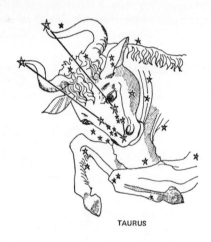

TAURUS

Taurus the Bull (21 April to 21 May)
Basically your nature is restful, phlegmatic, patient, even inclined to idleness, but it is part of you to acquire wealth and possessions because these are the *fodder* you need for the quiet life; your philosophy is to live and let live. You will almost slave to death to get money to achieve your aims. When aroused from your calm (or lethargy as some might call it) you often behave like a bull in a china shop.

To rob a Taurean of possessions is almost to attack him physically. As every *matador* knows, the bull is a gentle, peaceful creature until provoked. You like harmony and beauty in people; you are conventionalists.

You are slow thinkers and slow movers and dislike violence, brutality and revolutions. You can sometimes become so conservative as to be immobile, but you have tremendous reserves of energy for anything that you firmly believe in or support : this can be a weakness because it may lead to the very extremes of egoism.

You are as much the victim of habit as a creature thereof. Wine, love and song are much enjoyed by Taureans, you are usually sensual and inclined to indulge your emotions – sometimes too much for your own good.

It is extremely important to help Taurus children build up solid, reliable and socially acceptable habits. Taureans without ingrained good habits may easily develop bad habits. No Taurean can endure emotional, financial, intellectual or philosophical uncertainty. Some will immerse themselves in any dogma or -ism just to provide themselves with a feeling of security.

As regards taste in furnishings, literature, music and painting the Taurean leans to the classical styles in preference to the vogue of the moment. Many Taureans are gourmets. Only in one things are Taurus folk poor connoisseurs – their fellow human beings. Their failures in human relationship may make Taureans very bitter, often so contrary that they may deliberately refuse help to those in need, but give generously to those who don't need it. Failure is something that Taurus often invites by bad public relations. Failure makes the Taurus tyrannical and harsh. Often even in later success, bitterness may linger on – hence the temperamental opera-singers, the fiery tempered conductors etc. who are often found in this group.

It is strange how the softness, gentleness and good nature of Taurus can so often become blunted and distorted.

GEMINI

Gemini the Twins (22 May to 20 June)

What genius, what inventiveness, what talent you Gemini people display! How often you waste it with shallowness, pseudo-intellectualism! Only those of you who reach the height of world-fame show the world what wonders Gemini can reach. Too often you defend brilliantly an argument as an exercise and not because you really believe in it; in this way you may get a reputation for shallowness and insincerity. You easily lose interest in things. Admittedly you are some of the world's greatest enthusiasts, but however much you believe in an idea you are liable to change. You do not very much like to keep one steady job – boredom is a living death to you. It is a pity, because you are usually good, hard and steady workers.

Somewhere deep down in Gemini people is a love of reason, sense, logic and wisdom. You are practical fast workers, down-to-earth and quick-witted. You make yourselves very useful to other people (especially business and organisations) and as such quickly become very popular, often achieving lightning promotion.

Gemini's weakness is in spreading the load of genius into too many different interests, too many hobbies, too many fields of interest. You are pliable, adaptable people, fairly easy to get on with. Aquarians (positive) fascinate you, inspire you and often bring out the best in you.

You thoroughly enjoy clubs, gatherings and the social aspects of society. You have your own ideas and can be very firm in seeing them through – so long as you don't change horses in midstream.

So often the life-and-soul-of-the-party, the Gemini can nevertheless experience low-points of loneliness and sorrow, but rarely for long. You do not usually adhere to morals, customs or beliefs which you do not value, which get in your way or from which you have been converted.

Your nerves are often shot-to-pieces through lack of rest, overwork or over-excitement. Under such conditions you are liable to smoke, or drink too much or become the victim to drugs. Gemini people rarely rest enough or relax easily.

You have artistic talents in almost any field, but must be patient enough to master the techniques of it before you can show what abilities you have.

You are frequently careless drivers on the road, whether using a car, bicycle or even a donkey-cart! Without self-discipline in such things you can rob the world of your contributions to society before you start! You are fundamentally extroverts and seldom make friends with introverts. As Gemini can, at will, tell lies without a blush, often he relates truth to the hard line of necessity rather than to the facts. *There dwell two souls within my breast* as Goethe's Faust said.

You love travel for its change and excitement.

At your best you are a boon to Mankind, at your worst far, far below such a standard.

Cancer the Crab (21 June to 22 July)
For many this is a truly deceptive sign. You so often appear hard, tough, resilient but within your own personalities there are both gentleness and softness in abundance. The sad thing is that others often hurt you far more than they

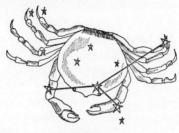

CANCER

know. They take a sledgehammer to crack a nut, and
instead of just a slap your friends may so hurt your pride
and self-respect as to lose you for good. This is a pity
because few signs are so emotionally rich and sincere. You
are deeply sensitive, easily moved by not only personal
experiences but by things you read and hear about from
others. How easily tears and laughter may come to you.
Cancer people require a home, a retreat, a shelter, a den –
somewhere safe to hide from the world and all that troubles
you. You love home, garden, family and comfort. Your
gentle nature is such that many things trouble you – other
people, business, money and your health – do take care
not to become a hypochondriac! The trouble is that you
tend to be pessimistic. Too frequently you look on the
black side of things. You can get real success in life only
when you overcome your pessimistic tendencies.

Your fundamental existence is tied to your emotions,
to your inner world; it is often to you that friends and
relatives – even strangers – entrust their secrets. Alas, when
you want to confide in others it is often you that get let
down and betrayed. The Cancer subject is very conscious
of his or her self respect – and the just respect of others;
to lose either is hell for you.

Another thing that causes you pain is any violence,
brutality, vandalism, mockery; even raw bad manners make
your lips curl with disgust.

You Cancer-born people often keep silent rather than

argue. Inexperienced folk may think your silence is stupidity – far from it, you think and bide your time.

Your common weakness is a marked dependence upon the opinions of others, but this is linked to your emotional entanglements.

You Cancer types love facts and logic but are frequently illogical in your own behaviour. Your memory is often prodigious; very often you link material to be learnt with your emotions, which makes for pleasant learning! You like to be treated sensibly and logically, but you often follow sudden impulses – you are the last people to realise that this sort of thing makes you difficult to understand. Strangely enough, you sometimes feel too embarrassed to offer help or advice because you feel that this interferes with the private life of another – and such interference is generally unwelcome to you yourself.

Loved ones and friends can give the Cancer-born few kindnesses better than privacy, a chance to retreat, to disappear, to think and meditate. Nobody can ever fully ' possess ' a Cancer person – one may only love as much of their personality as they let emerge from their ' shell '.

You tend to fight (mentally) by force of inertia, by steady, unflagging resistance rather than by sheer will-power and brute force; you believe (often vainly) that other people will eventually follow logic and behave decently.

You value freedom greatly but frequently preserve it best in a family circle. You are very slow and careful in making friends but you tend to keep the friends you make. You expect new acquaintances to give proof of good intent before you regard them as friends. Affection is never enough; you insist upon respect for your personality and ideas as well. Your anxiety concerning what others say about you is such that you prefer to be insulted to your face than slighted behind your back.

It is extremely dangerous for Cancer people to drink as a flight from reality: Alcohol as a habit is the fatal beginning of the end for you. Drugs are even more fatal – Cancer folk too easily become addicts.

You often have exceptional talent in political work. You have a powerful understanding of the occult and are often clairvoyant; you can often deal with others by telepathy.

You usually like travel, especially by water. Almost always Cancer people love water, boats, fishing, living by the sea, rivers, lakes etc. Most of you take your holidays by water or on the water.

If you make no attempt to carry out your dreams in some practical fashion you can collapse, degenerate and ruin yourselves.

Unfortunately, you are subject to moods and you do not react favourably to the urgings of friends who try to encourage you to work for your goals.

LEO

Leo the Lion (23 July to 22 August)

Well-named the lion, because your nature has something royal about it when it is at its best. At all times you have an instinct for leadership, for responsibilities, for making decisions (not that yours are always right) because you have that feeling for judgment, determination and government. You suffer from frustration more than many other birth-signs because your natural instincts for this predominance are allowed few outlets.

One drawback is that although you have the instincts for leadership you often lack the will to work for it. It is not really that you are lazy, it is that your mind tends to wander to bigger issues, and you prefer to leave the usual (and essential) tasks of everyday life to others.

There is a sense of nobility in your character, and your friends and relatives may often exploit this to your cost. Honour and honourable behaviour go with your lordly concept of what a leading figure in the world should be. You trust others sometimes to the point of sheer stupidity, seldom believing gossip, preferring to have the hard experience of knowing for yourself . . . but then it is finished. Once betrayed, your rage is royal and reconciliation almost unthinkable. You like straight thinking, never shirking a battle, you prefer an open disagreement to deceit; in the words of the Italian proverb you *prefer an open war to a pretended peace.*

To say you are extrovert is an understatement; you make superlative actors, and do not keep all your acting to the stage. Sometimes you fail to realise that friends and family see through some of your bluff and play-acting (face it, you do indulge in it) and this explains the sarcasm and scorn you sometimes receive from them, so next time you think you're in hot water think before you roar at them – you could have made some error, overstepped the mark and failed them! Boast, if you must, but preferably after your achievements, not before them.

Use your tremendous energy and will-power to persevere until you obtain your desired goals.

Luxury is almost an essential to Leos, and somewhere in your life you must have a little quiet luxury, it belongs to the superbly self-confident egoism you practise.

Most Leos are very charming, well-behaved, elegant and fond of formality, etiquette, politeness, traditions etc.

You can seldom resist an argument or a fight, but you tend to fight fairly on the whole; so much cannot be said for several other birthsigns.

Leos are often taken in by flattery and ruined by adherence to *good causes* which advance somebody else's interests more than their own, but their sense of right and decency is such that you seldom suspect what depths others may go down to.

In the right post you make wonderful people to work for and show a generosity and understanding to those beneath you which makes you very popular.

VIRGO

Virgo the Virgin (23 August to 22 September)
You are one of the most mature of all birthsigns; even as children you seem wise, prudent and mature long before anybody could expect it of you.

Nobody fazes you, you are unflappable, imperturbable. You keep calm, cool, you think, make decisions. You have orderly, calculating minds; you love system, cleanliness, perfection and all that keeps to the rules. Aquarians worry you, however much you are fascinated with them, and Librans do not do you much good. Your emotional life is very much subject to your intelligence – and this last is a keyword of your lives. As well as exceptionally beautiful people such as Greta Garbo (the Swedish actress whose charm was proverbial) you also number Michael Faraday – the chemist, physicist and discoverer of the conduction of electrical current (thus making it a commercial practicality) among your illustrious group.

Your love of organisation, cleaning-up, systemising and so on is occasionally overdone, if you are not careful it can become a vice and make everybody else around you really miserable.

You criticise and analyse too much; try not to make it so terribly public! Because you find punctuality easy do not think it is one of the seven deadly sins for others who are not so fortunate.

You are very dependent upon the opinions of others, but quick to discern flattery from the real thing.

You very often end up as specialist in some subject or other that appeals to you, and a lot of Virgos have been found among world authorities in certain fields of study. You do not usually approve of occult things (including astrology or palmistry) but if you do study them you can become very expert in them.

Loneliness is the curse of your sign; to be alone is terrible for you; you need others around you to mother them, serve them, help them, and you feel lost without people. You are so practical, so ready to help and so capable, it is a shame that your inner reserve is often mistaken for coldness. This is tragic, because the love that is in you can rarely find a full outlet; people see the cold, calculating efficiency, the intellect and often miss the sincerity and affection that is within you.

So sad is your experience of life that frequently you for-swear joy and pleasure, and become puritanical.

You are at your best when you find a really good mate in life. When your emotional life is secure you can do wonders.

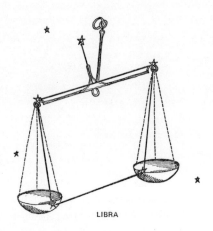

LIBRA

Libra the Scales (23 September to 22 October)
You are concerned with balance, and sometimes so wish to bring things (and other people, of course) into a correct balance that you crash something down heavily on one scale to bring the other up into line – frequently too heavily. You have tremendous talent but are often more heavyhanded than you know in dealing with other people. In your search for a perfect balance you perhaps miss out on the idea that if everything were equal the universe would be a flat, uninteresting plain without a bush in sight.

You are very peaceful by nature, and will do much to avoid trouble – up to a certain point. Then you can go in with heavy hands to restore what you see as the correct balance, surprising people with the severity of your fighting spirit.

You like life to be rhythmic, full of decent compromise and harmony. You are superb dancers, musicians (your sense of time is so good). You become intoxicated with beauty, and sullen, disappointed and introvertedly unhappy if you are deprived of it.

You can be extraordinarily lazy, and many of you could achieve more of the luxury and beauty you long for if you set to, made clothes, hats, painted pictures, made furniture and created what you want . . . there are plenty of books on instruction in all the world's libraries, your talent is such that you can succeed in almost any artistic field you study.

Working and studying do come harder than just admiring beauty. When Librans can pull themselves out of the rut of doing nothing they can succeed brilliantly. You are smooth talkers, diplomats all, flatterers, and flirts. You have an overwhelming sense for the romantic, a deep need to be loved flamboyantly and demonstratively : To be given a small and simple present by one you love in the midst of a crowded restaurant – where everybody can see it – is more important than some very expensive gift bestowed in private !

No sign can listen so intently to the sorrows, problems and gossip of others; your curiosity is catlike, and quite insatiable, you have a curious love of seemingly unimportant details, and will often interrupt a narrative with a totally irrelevant question such as *What was the colour of the ribbon on the hem of her dress?* or *Did the arrows on his tie point upwards or downwards?* Such questions are liable to bring apoplexy to Aquarians and other signs who concern themselves with wide issues, cosmic plans etc. But such details are really quite important to your index-card memory.

Whatever you say, your real happiness is linked to a love-life on an even keel, and you do not really blossom out with dramatic grand passionate love affairs, they merely throw you off balance. Elegance, manners, courtesy and beauty are your birthright, and you could make a comfortable and chic home out a barn.

Nothing is so bad for Librans as to be deprived of the

C

company and friendship of their fellow-men and women. You must belong to clubs, societies etc. to be happy and successful.

You may complain without end about conditions but your ability to adapt to almost anything is remarkable. You are gamblers by instinct, but often suffer from deep-rooted insecurity which robs you of much success. Your artistic and dramatic instincts often incline you to exaggerate misfortunes and dwell upon injustices too long.

Often possessed of grace and beauty, always capable of extraordinary charm, you get away with a lot of things no other birthsign would try on.

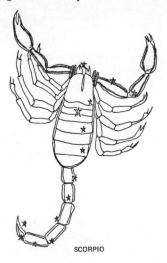

SCORPIO

Scorpio the Scorpion (23 October to 21 November)
What a mixed people you Scorpions are! What other sign could produce Katherine Hepburn and Martin Luther? To say nought of Trotsky and St. Augustine! The differences may be many, but the similarity lies in this, each of them is a fighter, each of the seeming extremes has courage, determination and a will not to give in.

You are a people who dislike compromise; Librans

Cancer, and Aquarians irritate you with their tendency to work out clever, intricate face-saving devices. You like a world of simple, easy-to-recognise blacks and whites. You prefer to say what you think, often never reflecting what damage it can do to others. Your weakness is a tendency to regard your own opinions as nigh infallible. More tact could broaden your circle of friends. You too easily feel attacked by others, under criticism, under fire, and so you react and attack back (you call it self-defence). At your worst you become spiteful, petty and nurse revenge for real or imagined slights too long for your own good.

To think coolly is difficult for Scorpios, so often emotions rise up to torment you, so often it seems as if every hand is turned against you. In view of the sarcasm and satire of which most of you are capable it would not be surprising if this were sometimes the case. You just fail to realise how hard you sting. Too often you base your life upon some inalienable *Truth* or doctrine – as did the late Senator McCarthy of the witch-hunt fame in USA, and the un-lamented Dr. Goebbels. There is only your doctrine, and the wrong ones (i.e. anything else that is not yours).

Boredom, cowardice, passivity, privilege, and many other things are a source of annoyance to you – although you have nothing against any privileges you possess your-selves. You make the best detectives (if you can keep your cool) and for that matter secret agents, and a number of world famous generals have been born under Scorpio. The strange thing is that you wilt and decay if there are no difficulties to overcome. Some Scorpios are exceptionally weak, helpless and negative within their own sign, and then the worst thing to do is to point out to them their own weakness, it is something Scorpios can never forgive.

Applying all this fantastic, aggressive power to problems of science, mathematics, space-travel and so on makes Scorpios among the benefactors of Mankind, they never let a problem beat them . . . as witness Madame Curie, the discoverer of radium.

Scorpios must educate themselves; their greatest possible danger lies in lack of knowledge, without education a Scorpio is doomed to failure, bitterness and despair. Each Scorpio has only one real enemy – himself. Strangely enough you do not quarrel with other Scorpios. Scorpio can wed Scorpio with more peace and happiness than almost any other sign wedding within the sign.

Until you achieve self-discipline and education you do not stand a chance of success, and you should give up every project until you have achieved these two essentials.

SAGITTARIUS

Sagittarius the Archer (22 November to 20 December)
Warm and sympathetic people, good mixers, fond of company, popular, kind and fond of helping others: Those are the nice things about Sagittarians.

You like to shoot your arrows straight, to come to the point, not to beat about the bush. You are impulsive, makers of quick decisions (often regretted at leisure), there is a touch of the hero and the martyr in your make-up (hence the ironical French newspapers' slur that General de Gaulle fancied himself as a second Joan of Arc).

Your sign is shown shooting an arrow heavenwards. This is precisely the tune of Sagittarians, you have a whole part of your nature which is orientated towards the spiritual, the metaphysical, the mental, the unknown world.

Many of you paint; some of the greatest religious painters of the world have been Sagittarians.

You have much about you that leans to philosophy and dreaming. You love the wild and primitive places, you long for a quiet beach, a coral strand with palms and a soft surf, or for a desolate mountain track. You make magnificent veterinary surgeons. Few people understand and love animals as you do – and you can love them without making semi-humans out of them. At your worst you can become like animals yourself, gruff, brutish, raw, untamed, fierce and ready to fight. At your best the energy you are possessed of can make you charming, great, noble benefactors to the human race.

Normally you have a deep sense of honour, and like to keep your promises. You like all to be open, honest, upright and most of your life you try to behave that way yourself.

Although you normally dislike affectation you have a weakness for courtly ceremonies, traditions and rituals.

You would rather spend your all on one or two genuine objects of art than have a mass of imitations around you; this goes for your attitude to friendships too.

Justice, morality and honour are usually key thoughts in your relationships to other people and life generally. You do not keep secrets well, and blurt out the truth as if your life depended upon it.

Many think you are lucky; actually you are highly intuitive. You have a flair for the occult sciences, and may be able to use them very efficiently, partly because you have a flair for distinguishing the genuine from the false.

You are always adventurous, fond of travel; liberty is essential to you; you are in all things magnanimous even to your enemies. Many signs may find you tactless – you must be careful not to lose friends by frankness.

Capricorn the Goat (21 December to 19 January)

Few birthsigns master their own emotions so well as Capricorns; sometimes their emotions are so well under control as to be nigh invisible to other signs, and poor Capricorns are consequently often misunderstood.

CAPRICORN

You are so capable of living alone that it is sometimes difficult for you to admit people into your inner life. You do not advertise your emotions; few people appreciate how deep and sincere you almost inarticulate people can be.

It is said of Capricorn children that they are born old, and the gaiety, spontaneity, joy and happiness which other people can turn on like the switch of a light are difficult for you; you do not forget your problems, your sorrows, your troubles so easily.

You are not gamblers but you believe in luck when it happens to you. You are steady plodders. Many people think you are pessimistic; this is not true, it is just that you have your nose to the grindstone so close that you can rarely think beyond one step at a time.

Fame, popularity, and the wide esteem of all who know you come more easily than riches to you – often because you cannot grasp out so adventurously as other signs might for wealth within your reach. Your virtues are those of regularity, punctuality, industriousness, thoroughness, conscientiousness. You make school teachers, civil servants, lawyers, historians and scientists.

You suffer from depression especially if your love is not returned (often you idolise a person who will unwittingly hurt you, who is really wrong for you). You are not really happy in company, clubs, associations, you like people in ones or twos – you are not the ideal cocktail party socialiser.

You do not show thoughts, especially to superiors, but have every intention of butting them from behind if you catch them bending after they have played dirty on you. Pride is a fault among you; one has to be very tactful indeed to guide, help or encourage you – all offers can be accepted except those which destroy your self-respect or independence. You need sympathy and understanding very much, but may get little until you mellow with age when it is easier to see your good points.

You tire little from the tasks you set yourself, tire not at all from a goal you wish to reach, but do not set too many goals in life for yourself.

You are better at defence than attack, and prefer to be left in peace best of all.

Aquarius the Waterbearer (20 January to 18 February)
There are two types of Aquarians. In no other sign is the positive and negative so different – the negative is sleepy, lazy and full of unfulfilled dreams . . . with luck this develops in later life to the positive type, concerning whom the following is written.

In no other sign are so many geniuses, poets, philosophers, inventors and actors born. The Aquarian is above all by very nature an actor, and it is difficult to know what is the true Aquarian and what is an act – sometimes you yourselves don't know. You effervesce, sparkle, dazzle and bewilder friends and foes alike. You ooze charm, but can be

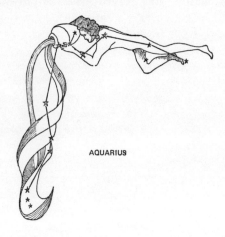

AQUARIUS

one of the cruellest and most ruthless of all signs when aroused. Luckily your anger is like a summer storm, noisy, terrible, but soon gone.

The world lives on your ideas, seldom bothering to give you credit for them. Probably only Leos will reward you justly for your efforts on their behalf. Gemini will marry you (or live with you) and Scorpios will want to attack your sparkling unorthodoxy. It often seems that Aquarians are unorthodox out of sheer perversity; actually you are often so spiritually far ahead of your times that others seldom see your visions, understand the logic of what you do . . . or trust you.

You are more than dreamers or optimists, you are discoverers, explorers, inventors par excellence. Your capacity for hard work (if anything YOU want to do) is prodigious.

Truly speaking, your sign carries water, it is an AIR sign NOT a water sign at all. People who attack you find it like punching a ball of smoke, what they mistake to be your weakest point is often merely part of a meaningless façade which you have erected (how well you can live a part) and which you discard or lose without a second thought. You are not vicious, but can be pitiless fighters if angered. Your tolerance is often mixed with disdain and contempt; you are sometimes so intellectually advanced that you scorn to take action on those who are hurting you. Some of the world's greatest writers have been Aquarians, your talent in this field is without equal. Edison, of whom it is said no man on earth invented or discovered more, was an Aquarian who had his head read by a phrenologist, was told he had inventive talent and set out to prove it.

You are the unlikely people who set forth to put your dreams and ideals into practical form, beneficial to all others of the human race.

You do not always reach the top or attain fame (unless after death) because you cannot endure routine, office hours, regularity or punctuality. You never disguise your contempt of stupidity, and frequently lack tact at a critical moment. You are fascinating, charming and yet often remain single; you never tire of your own company and thoughts.

You probe into the unknown, including the occult and mystic side of life, with a serious, scientific and curious approach. Often Aquarians achieve such a mastery of occult sciences as to scare less-informed mortals. You love to be well dressed, but as often as not spend much of your day in informal clothes, track-suit, jeans, etc.

If you study and learn to overcome the tendency to be merely dilettante you will go far in the world. You desire to crowd many experiences into your lives, to learn and experience all you possibly can, and you often feel that if you put yourself 100% into any one thing there will be nothing of you left over for anything else – indeed, you may be right. You love deeply, are frequently heartbroken and often betrayed. Aquarians at their most positive and enlightened are like people from an older, wiser planet, *starborn*; at best you are a puzzle to all you meet. Gemini and Cancer understand you best, and with others the more you understand to read character the less hurt you will be.

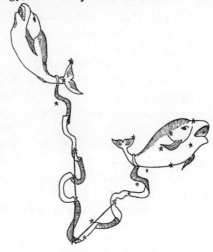

PISCES

Pisces the Fish (19 February to 20 March)

In the sign there are two fish; each points in a different direction. This is the curse of Pisceans, always there seems a dilemma, always two possibles, and resulting indecision. Not even sure of your own nature you are one of the most difficult of all signs to understand; how can one possibly interpret your desires and wishes when you are not really sure what you want.

You are outspoken but very emotional, too much so in many cases for your own happiness. You philosophise deeply over unimportant things, and only by developing a well-founded education can you offer the world the talent which lies at your disposal. You are fundamentally altruistic and very inclined to risk your luck, play a hunch. Much to the annoyance of your more logical friends you often pull it off. Perhaps you have an instinctive understanding of the laws of chance . . . you are usually good at mathematics in any form. You find all water sports fascinating. You flirt with the occult but are often sceptical intuitively. Logic is not your strongest point, some of you achieve more than others there, but not too often. Music is a strong point with you, under Pisces both Chopin and Albert Einstein were born!

Pisces must take care never to become addicts of anything, alcohol or drugs . . . for you may often verge upon the incurable if it becomes a form of flight from reality. Indeed you are strongly recommended to keep to the safer forms of healing such as herbalism, homoeopathy, etc. Many forms of state medicine employ drugs which can lead to addiction by Pisceans.

So often you feel buffeted too much by this world, and allow yourselves to be driven hither and thither with a really negative hopelessness, your only hope is to discipline yourself, force yourself into the positive thinking attitudes that alone can make you a successful, happy person.

Males and females are often remarkably beautiful and attractive people, be careful who you marry, a wrong alliance can bring you to the depths of despair.

You are very much creatures of habit, make sure that such habits as you form are positive ones leading to further uplift and enlightenment.

You are suckers for a hardluck story, do watch that you don't beggar yourselves!

Generosity is a fault with you; often you can't stop yourself from giving.

Your bearing is often remarkably stately, you have a natural dignity which makes you much respected as parents. For a really happy home life and marriage the indications are that no sign will suit you quite so well as Cancer.

In argument you are easily convinced, but never held for long. You will nearly always revert back to your own original opinions.

You are one of the most forgiving and tender of all birthsigns, and hate practically nobody, and almost nothing except hatred and violence. In any religion you make gentle, pastoral priests with a delicate understanding and love of your fellow human beings.

Chapter 2

The Zodiac and your Love Life

Love is a reality which is born in the fairyland of Romance
said Talleyrand; let none of us deny that under natural
circumstances there are few emotions or human activities
which take up so much of our time.

In *Iphigenia auf Tauris* Goethe's character says:— *My
life began only when I first loved you* – what a wise, mature
and beautiful thought!

How much each of us owes to the love of others in our
lives. Why, then, is some love creative and beautiful, other
love destructive and bitter?

The American actor Pete Duel said: *Love is the only
thing you must earn, everything else you can steal.*

Is it not likely that in our eagerness, in our blindness, we
overlook simple, obvious home-truths, things of which we
may say *The fault lies not in our stars, dear Brutus, but in
ourselves.*

Details of the mistakes we can make are explained simply
in this section. It does not follow that you will definitely
have sorrow or disappointment if you are married to a
partner who is astrologically unsuitable because there are
such factors as ascendants, cusps, which may lessen or
intensify certain traits.

When your ruling planet is exalted in a certain sign it is
clear that you can benefit from such influences in more
ways than one. It is commonly believed that Mars and

Pluto form a combination which can bring nothing but tragedy to the partners.

In the *Marienbader Elegie* which Goethe wrote at about the age of 80, the immortal lover, that gentle kindly and sensuous prince of poets, wrote:—

> *To love and be loved in return*
> *is the greatest joy on Earth*

This prized possession can belong to each and every one of us if we take the trouble to balance our love life and sexual inclinations by the advice of the horoscope. Usually the opposite partner of the sign of the Zodiac is beautifully balanced, for you, and even to the extent of matching your sexual needs and inclinations. As a rough guide remember that six months away from your own birth date is a handy reference.

Male signs are considered to be Aquarius, Aries, Gemini, Leo, Libra, Sagittarius.

Female signs are Cancer, Capricorn, Pisces, Scorpio, Taurus and Virgo.

This does not mean that persons tend to be effeminate or masculine if born in an opposite group, only that men born in one group are very much male, and women born in the other very female. The Sun is held to be masculine as a sign : The Moon feminine.

As regards the other planets :—

Venus – Feminine, sign of romantic, sensuous love.

Mars – Male, virile, dashing sexuality.

Uranus – Bisexual, positive, attractive and magnetic.

Neptune – Bisexual, negative, passive.

Pluto – Masculine, nervous, neurotic even, passive.

Jupiter – Masculine, positive, optimistic, law-abiding.

Mercury – Somewhat neuter, very communicative, lovers under this sign have a great facility of communication with one another.

Aries (21 March to 20 April)
You need a mate who is adaptable, capable of total surrender, very fair, just, able to make allowances, charming, even-tempered, and under Venus. Avoid exploiting your partner. Injustice will destroy your mate's love for you. Tactlessness will wound far more than Aries lovers realise.

Avoid: Capricorn, Cancer and other Aries – too quarrelsome.

Seek: Leo or Sagittarius. Possible happiness with Gemini, Libra or Aquarius.

Under Mars: Exalted in Capricorn.

Taurus (21 April to 21 May)
You need a very full, ardent and sexually active partner, free of guilt complexes. Your mate must be very sexually and emotionally mature. You need love to be shown and proved by acts, deeds and life, not by Italian medieval love poems, and presents of aftershave lotions. Taurus people desperately need love and fulfilment. They need dynamic mates who will give and take as heartily and sincerely as they do themselves.

Avoid: Very possessive or shallow people. Avoid fellow Taurus folk. Scorpio subjects will break your heart.

Seek: Capricorn or Virgo. Possible happiness with Pisces or Cancer.

Under Venus: Exalted in Pisces.

Gemini (22 May to 20 June)
Your mate should be active, fond of travel and novelty, a rugged hearty outdoor type. You need a happy-go-lucky adventurer, the cheerful, bounce-back-again personality. Nevertheless you need a partner with intellect and capacity to learn well. You can be very happily married to the right partner.

Avoid: Pisces and Virgo.

Seek : Aquarius and Libra. Other Gemini people are rarely
more than a passing fancy.

Under Mercury : Exalted in Venus.

Cancer (21 June to 22 July)

You need a disciplined, conscientious, stable and steady
partner. Someone who is devoted to a cause, an ideal, or
a good, worthwhile job. Usually inclined to marry tradi-
tionalists. You like fun but tire quickly of stupid frivolity.
You need a partner who likes water and water sports. Your
mate needs be keen on economic stability and a social
climber.

Avoid : Aries, Libra and other Cancer people.

Seek : Pisces and Scorpio.

Affairs : often with Capricorns.

Under Moon : Exalted in Taurus.

Leo (23 July to 22 August)

Your partner needs be very adaptable to change, able to
take hardship when some of your grandiose schemes fall
flat. Tact, warmth, tenderness and acceptance of your
leadership is required. The right mate is the key to success
for Leo people. Your partner needs courage – to stand up
to you. There must be sufficient hunger for love to match
your own needs.

Avoid : Taurus and Scorpio.

Seek : Aries, Sagittarius, Gemini and Libra. Affairs with
Aquarius but seldom permanent happiness. Leo is mysti-
fied by the depths of the Aquarian soul.

Under Sun : Exalted in Aries.

Virgo (23 August to 22 September)

You need a partner who can show some mystique, charm
and fascination; an idealist, slightly psychic perhaps, somebody with enough imagination to match your tremendous
practicality and pragmatism. You are often a materialist,
your mate needs be almost impractical; this may be mad-

dening but never boring. Better still if the mate is musically inclined to bring you solace after your labours. You need a sensitive, tender, loving person. Avoid hurting your mate by sheer carelessness and brashness.

Avoid : Sagittarius, Leo, Aries and Gemini.

Seek : Other Virgo people, Taurus and Capricorns. You can never understand Aquarius or Libra well.

Libra (23 September to 22 October)

You need a strong mate : you rarely forgive weakness except in yourself! Your own often well-concealed insecurity demands a Mars governed partner. The less flexible and more domineering your mate the more you idolise this person. You make an excellent second-in-command to a bold, visionary, enthusiast, Librans like extremely male or wholly female personalities accordingly : you can be bitter, ruthless and unfeeling towards anybody who falls short of your standard.

Avoid : Other Libra people. You are intolerant of Capricorn and usually approach them the wrong way.

Seek : Gemini, Sagittarius or Leo; occasionally Cancer. You tend to fail Aquarians and hurt them.

Under Venus : Exalted in Pisces.

Scorpio (23 October to 21 November)

You need a person whose sexual responses are rapid and willing, a pleasure-loving happy mate. Such people may become a clinging vine which you often despise but secretly treasure. You are liable to arouse opposition in your loved one; do not be spiteful or careless in what you say or do. Your partner will most likely row with you, but almost certainly stay loyal to you.

Avoid : Leo, Taurus and Aquarius.

Seek : Cancer, Pisces and Virgo – also other Scorpios. You are rarely 100% faithful except to Cancer and Pisces.

Under Pluto : Exaltation is debated.

Sagittarius (22 November to 20 December)
You will most likely choose a modest but carefree mate. This must be a person who can hold your interest and change mood to match your own. You are happiest with people under Mercury, because you need a spontaneous response to your thoughts and your sexuality.

Avoid: Other Sagittarius, Virgo and Pisces.

Seek: Aries and Leo. While Aquarius and Librans attract you it is difficult to be loyal to them.

Under Jupiter: Exalted in Cancer.

Capricorn (21 December to 19 January)
You need an idealist, a sympathetic loyal love who will not rub your nose in the dirt when you make mistakes or do something stupid. You need a good, clean homely background to give you strength. Nagging robs you of success. You can break the heart of an ill-matched mate. You need a calm, contemplative and good-looking mate to support you and build up your frequent lack of confidence.

Avoid: Cancer, Scorpio and be careful of Libra relationships.

Seek: Capricorns, Taurus and Virgo. You will be charmed by but rarely satisfied by Aquarians.

Aquarians (20 January to 18 February)
It is strange that you who are basically selfless often find a self-centred mate. Aquarians mother or father their partners, but like to see some aspirations, imagination, solidity and moral fibre. You do not object to fireworks or dramatics so long as there is love, vitality, loyalty and a little mystique and charm. You are an exceptionally hard zodiac sign to love and understand. You attract many who do not always stay the course. Many Aquarians are elegant and chic, love romance and are liable to lose themselves in love.

Avoid: Other Aquarians, Aries, Pisces.

Seek: Gemini, Cancer and Taurus. Aquarians often have

D

many love affairs and make good teachers of love and
life.

Under Uranus : Exalted in Scorpio.

Pisces (19 February to 20 March)

You need a very lively and efficient partner full of enthusiasm and able to endure your blacker, more pessimistic
periods of doubt and perplexity. Your mate will be able to
stop and think when you feel rash or to urge you on when
you hesitate on the brink of success. You need a home-lover
and home-builder. You love practical realists.

Avoid : Gemini, Virgo, Sagittarius and other Pisces.

Seek : Cancer, Scorpio, Taurus, also occasionally Capricorn.

Under Neptune : Exaltation is debatable.

Chapter 3

How to Get the Best out of your Health with Astrology

This section about your health also gives advice on what sort of doctor the different signs of the Zodiac can produce . . . and you will be able to find which type of doctor is likely to help you best. Do not forget that it may be advisable to choose an adviser born six months away from your own sign.

There are few things in the world which are as important as our health. We all know that mentally and physically we need good health to feel our best.

If there is some indication of the likely pitfalls to which our birth sign renders us prone we can the more easily take precautions to avoid the dangers. It is rather like driving a car along the road; if there are clear road signs we can foresee dangers, and being forewarned slow down and take avoiding action.

It may be possible by a careful study of astrology to make your life happier, and healthier.

Health may be made better by using herbs for such everyday things as wines, beers, cosmetics, medicines, cooking aids etc. One of the things which all signs of the Zodiac appreciate is the value of simple, natural medicines which have been used with safety for many centuries – as opposed to one or two years of highly publicised over-advertised and excessively expensive man-made drugs about which too little is known.

Many useful herbs can be grown in gardens or even in window-boxes; and the leaves and bark of many familiar trees and shrubs can also be utilised as medical preparations.

The information contained in this section must be read carefully and intelligently. Where I have noted that one sign may be inclined to develop rheumatic illnesses this does not mean that everybody born under that sign will definitely get a rheumatic illness; it means that they must take great care to avoid conditions and dietetic faults which could lead to that condition.

Conversely, it does not mean that a person will not take some injury or illness because it is not common in his or her sign. The radiesthesists have shown that certain vibrations predominate in certain places, and that these can affect whosoever lives there. One of the dangers of man-made medicine is that its ingredients are artificial, and as such do not fall easily under natural planetary influences, so their effects on people are unpredictable. I have especially mentioned herbal medicine because this has often been linked with astrology by authorities in the past.

Nicholas Culpeper (1616–54), the Puritan herbalist, introduced a knowledge of astrology into medical work. He listed the plants in common use with their accepted planetary influences, and those are given in this section: he also used astrology for diagnosis.

Mankind has long been aware that the food we eat is related to health and energy. As we have grown more experienced we have come to make a distinguishing line between what is *food* and *nutrition*. That nutritive elements (proteins, enzymes, mineral salts and vitamins) are found in plants is natural; that healing which is directly linked with the natural processes (i.e. herbal treatment) must have priority is a logical follow-up. Dieticians have shown that most herbs are remarkably rich in nutritive elements, and many traditional treatments used from the days of Hippocrates (477–360 B.C.) contain all the necessary ingredients for a perfect dietetic cure of a specific condition.

To make certain that a safe cure is undertaken try to get a professional diagnosis of the condition.

ARIES

Aries (21 March to 20 April)
    (i)   You use up a tremendous amount of energy and often are unaware of tiredness until exhaustion sets in.
   (ii)   Usually neglect to seek medical advice.
  (iii)   Often accident prone.
  (iv)   Frequent high blood pressure in later years.
Seek : One whole free day and one free evening at least to relax in, free from work.
Avoid : (i) Quick, drastic changes of job or home. You need regular periods of peace and rest.
         (ii) Gobbling meals quickly. Alcohol is inadvisable in large quantities – it can destroy Aries subjects.
As a doctor : Especially for children and research. Practical and hardworking.

TAURUS

Taurus (21 April to 21 May)
    (i)   Tendency to exhaust yourself by burning the candle at both ends.

(ii)   Ear, nose and throat diseases are frequently met with in Taureans.

(iii)   Metabolism is often faulty, and varicose veins are frequently found.

Seek : Careful vitamin rich diet. Plenty of regular exercise, athletics and gymnastics (but don't overdo it).

Avoid : Putting on weight. Over-indulgence in drink. ' Manager complex ' (everything collapses without me). Depression and melancholia.

As a doctor : Conservative, methodical. Specialist in dietetics and running a convalescent home.

GEMINI

Gemini (22 May to 20 June)

(i)   Very subject to psycho-somatic illnesses; if you are unhappy you are most likely to show it in your bodily health.

(ii)   Strangely enough, Gemini people tend to suffer with bronchial and chest illnesses. But if you are in an accident it is most likely arms or legs that get hurt.

Seek : Careful, well-planned diets with special attention to vitamin B complex. Plenty of regular rest is essential.

Avoid : Skin and nerve troubles.

As a doctor : Best as analyst, psychiatrist, or general practitioner.

CANCER

Cancer (21 June to 22 July)

(i)   Stomach, colon, lymphatic and in feminine cancer

subjects menstruation disorders are fairly common.

(ii) Anaemia is often noticeable.

(iii) Subject often to obesity in later life.

(iv) Cancer folk sometimes *use* sickness to escape from some unpleasantness.

(v) Usually get 100% quicker results with herbal or occult remedies.

(vi) Take a midday nap if 30 years or older.

Avoid: (i) Food or drink which could upset bladder or kidneys.

(ii) Sleeping pills, all drugs, etc.

As a doctor: Excellent general practitioner. Good with children and old people. Also make good herbalists.

LEO

Leo (23 July to 22 August)

(i) Great general resistance to illness.

(ii) Tend to underestimate demands on your own strength. Rarely foresee pending exhaustion.

(iii) Heart and blood troubles can easily occur.

(iv) Weak back and intestines common.

Avoid: (i) Intestinal troubles. Leos sometimes become hypochondriacs, guard against this.

(ii) Getting fat.

As a doctor: Overwhelmingly ambitious. Exacting high standards for himself, nursing staff and patients.

VIRGO

Virgo (23 August to 22 September)
  (i)   Yours is not a very robust sign.
  (ii) Duodenal and other intestinal and stomach ailments are fairly common.
  (iii) From the list above it is clear that nervous upsets may develop, especially if there are dietetic irregularities.

Seek : Rest and emotional balance.

Avoid : Mental and emotional strains; beware of nervous exhaustion. Boredom is here often precursor of illness.

As a doctor : Good in research. Dogmatic but painstaking. Good bedside manner.

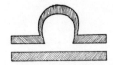

LIBRA

Libra (23 September to 22 October)
  (i)   Usually very poor reserves of energy, quickly depleted. This is disastrous for the nervous system. 8–9 hours sleep nightly is recommended.
  (ii) Kidneys, bladder, liver are often troublesome. All areas around the loins can give rise to anxiety. Diabetes and hernia are frequent among librans.
  (iii) Librans must never be allowed to brood over the past (or the present). This seriously affects their health.

Avoid : Brooding over past and present sorrows or nerves,

eyes and heart may suffer badly. All Librans need 8 hours sleep nightly.

As a doctor: Very keen on progressive treatments. Tends to live with problems 24 hours a day.

SCORPIO

Scorpio (23 October to 21 November)
  (i)   Scorpions seem to suffer frequently from illnesses linked to the lower parts of the abdomen, infections of urinary, rectal passages, of bladder etc.
  (ii) Very subject to dyspeptic and duodenal troubles of nervous origin – especially if members of administrative or executive staff.

Avoid: (i) Emotional and nervous upsets – these always tend to make you eat carelessly and induce imbalance of mineral salts and vitamins.

Avoid: (ii) Tranquillisers and drugs of all sorts most emphatically. There is some tendency to become addicted.

As a doctor: Dogmatic but very capable. General practitioner.

SAGITTARIUS

Sagittarius (22 November to 20 December)
  (i)   This is one of the strongest, healthiest and most sportive signs.
  (ii) There is a tendency to rheumatic and arthritic conditions.

(iii)   Muscle strain and injuries must be guarded against.
(iv)   Exhaustion is a frequent cause of nervous upset.

Avoid: Virus infections and neurotic tendencies.

As a doctor: Optimistic, kind, easy to talk to: Specialist for children, rehabilitation. Tends to overwork.

CAPRICORN

Capricorn (21 December to 19 January)

(i)   Usually you have a fairly solid resistance to illness. Capricorns do not like being sick and constantly belittle their symptoms. Consequently they rarely receive sufficient sympathy. Nerves often upset their internal organs.

(ii)   Bone structure, postural faults (hernia), skin, hair and nails must be guarded.

(iii)   Rest, uninterrupted meals and peaceful home life are essential.

Avoid: Stomach upsets by repressed nervous and allergy conditions.

As a doctor: Pioneer in new healing techniques. Good surgeons.

AQUARIUS

Aquarius (20 January to 18 February)

(i)   Most Aquarians live life to the full, tend to exhaust themselves, punish their bodies and ruin their nerves.

(ii)   Subject to poor blood circulation, lack of mineral salts and vitamin deficiency.

   (iii)   The nervous system must be taken care of.

   (iv)   There is a tendency to prefer natural healing methods. Weak ankles. Lymphatic disorders.

Avoid: Overwork, lack of sleep, rushing too much – from these simple causes many Aquarians become ill.

As a doctor: Deep concern for patients' health and welfare. Very conscientious and selfless. Gentle and easy to talk to. Quick to use any new proven technique. Remarkable abilities in herbal, homoeopathic healing, radiesthesia etc.

PISCES

Pisces (19 February to 20 March)

   (i)   Tend to suffer most from lymphatic and bronchial illnesses.

   (ii)   The blood must be kept pure and the nervous system well protected.

   (iii)   The feet are often a cause of trouble.

Avoid: High blood pressure and eye trouble due to worry and nervous causes.

As a doctor: Gentle general practitioners.

Chapter 4

How your Work can Bring you Happiness

The average man works eight hours a day, so most of us spend nearly one-third of our lives at work, whatever that work is.

With one-third of our life spent sleeping to recuperate the body from the exhaustion of the day, and one-third spent at work it is undeniable that the time spent earning our daily bread is going to project itself into the rest of our lives. A person who is happy in his (or her) work is a happy person to be with after work. A person suffering from injustices, ill-treatment, discontent at work cannot recover completely from such misery when he enters the doorway of his home; something of the sorrow lingers on.

Clearly it is to everybody's advantage to be happy in their work, and the choice of a career is all-important. Again, there is the case of a boss who wonders whether to give a man a chance to do a new job, give him a break. What sort of a risk is the boss going to take? Every man and woman likes to narrow down the odds in a gamble. This is just what this astrological guide might do for you when you are deciding on a career for yourself or your children, or pondering whether to give a person an opportunity to prove himself.

Every sign has its positive and its negative sides, and the remarks apply generally to the positive types . . . their manner of dress, their appearance, their speech tell us at once whether they are positive or negative.

Work, proclaimed the intrepid statesman von Humboldt, *is as needful to the human soul as food and drink to the body. No man likes to consider himself lazy.*

So much of our destiny lies within our own hands, shaping our own ends by our efforts and choices. If we take no care to seek what is the best for ourselves let us not blame God or other men for our disasters.

George Sand, illustrious French authoress, friend of Chopin and Alfred de Musset, declared: *Work is not Man's punishment, it is his reward and his strength, his glory and his pleasure.*

By care and thoughtful planning most of us can do something to re-plan our lives and make our work joyful.

CAREERS

Aries (21 March to 20 April)
You need a job with much freedom, not a lot of petty supervision, but independence of action. You work hard. Office jobs are quite unsuitable as is anything with a lot of routine. You enjoy jobs that bring you into contact with other people, but you do not fit too readily into teams, organisations and groups. You will tend to be respected for hard work and results but not well-loved by superiors.
Try: Travelling representative, open air work, or being your own master.

Taurus (21 April to 21 May)
You work at your best only if the background of home and emotional life are settled. If you can find a restful job which is in comfortable surroundings you work very well indeed. You have a great facility to spend money, you need it very badly and provided that your working conditions are right you can work yourself into the ground to get it. Horticulture, forestry and agriculture do not pay all that well but

Taurus do well in them. Success in luxury and artistic professions.

Gemini (22 May to 20 June)

People under this sign usually have brilliant intellectual capacity; clearly their work should be of a type that gives full range to their ability and remarkable enthusiasm for hard graft. Gemini people must avoid any work which is dull, monotonous, routine; they need freedom. Inventive, creative, full of initiative, Gemini people fit into almost any working group – although they may not always like them.

Cancer (21 June to 22 July)

Cancer folk drive themselves very efficiently; when they start something they invariably push it through to its finish. Usually this sign does its best when working alone or without direct supervision. Hotel and restaurant managers, café owners, swimming pool superintendents, shopkeepers and managers. Fashion work, scientific, photographic work – almost any serious, worthwhile job with an intellectual challenge and a chance of meeting and talking to people attracts Cancer types. Loyal and conscientious workers, Cancer is quickly put off by unfair treatment or bad conditions of work.

Leo (23 July to 22 August)

Your difficulty in work is that you feel instinctively and insistently that you should be at the top. Young Leo workers are often far too impatient. Leos never really enjoy working in a mass to be just a cog in a wheel; you must have a chance for good promotion. Brilliant organisers, you give orders far better than you take them, unless you respect the ability of your superiors.

Virgo (23 August to 22 September)

You usually prefer a job like the Civil Service or a similar occupation in which everything is set out in black and white. You need rules, fairness on both sides, and do well in scientific, technical and analytical work. You are clever in accountancy and all precise matters. You are not good in jobs where much imagination and initiative is required, although there is great talent in acting here. You make superb efficiency experts, but usually expect too much from other Zodiac signs.

Libra (23 September to 22 October)
You are not easy to place. You will often change a job according to emotional dictates. In art, music, ballet, exhibition-work, modelling, etc. you can excel. You co-operate marvellously with people you like, and might easily follow a favourite boss into another job – even if it meant a lower salary. You make sympathetic (if not always 100% faithful) bosses: Everyone comes to you with their tale of woe. You can be good diplomats and politicians. You can succeed in almost any work you undertake – provided you are emotionally happy.

Scorpio (23 October to 21 November)
You prefer work with a touch of adventure in it, with a chance to use your tact, charm and wit. Your natural fierce energy and your organising powers need a natural, healthy outlet. Chemists, dentists, doctors, car mechanics, professional soldiers, engineers; your talents are many. Many politicians and reformers are Scorpios.

Sagittarius (22 November to 20 December)
Intellectuals, farmers, electricians, inventors, many indeed are the fields of success available to Sagittarians – but not the Civil Service! You need freedom to move, to make responsible decisions and in which to bestow the benefits of your leadership. Any field of activity in which you serve a section of, or the entirety of, a community will make you very contented.

Capricorn (21 December to 19 January)
Among this sign are often found the quiet, efficient, over-modest experts. People will treasure your memory for years – which is just as well for you are seldom paid what you are worth. Albert Schweitzer, Heinrich Pestalozzi and Grock (the great clown) all made contributions of one sort or another to human happiness and welfare : they all died poor. You make superb schoolteachers, doctors, administrators, lawyers, historians, masseurs, and civil engineers. You desperately need security and are slow to act, slower to change jobs and slower to adapt : thus God created you – let none blame you if you differ from them. You work at a slower rhythm than most, and are easily misunderstood.

Aquarius (20 January to 18 February)
Yours is a fantastic sign. If you overcome the slow contemplation that more aggressive signs mistake for laziness you can show talent and sheer genius second to none. You can excel at anything and everything you put your mind to. In the non-biblical writings it is reported that Jesus taught : *This world is a bridge, do not build upon it.* Aquarians usually do not put themselves wholly 100% into anything – however good they are at it; there is always a deep occult awareness that life on earth is more than overspecialisation in one small field. There is no field of human endeavour in which Aquarians have not excelled and made a name for themselves. Your versatility is remarkable. In adaptability few people can match you. Tolerant bosses usually, you overwork yourselves more than you do others. The latest scientific fields are ideal for practical Aquarians; atomic, electric, space research etc. You cannot work if subjected to injustice or if unhappy in your job.

Pisces (19 February to 20 March)
Tireless workers, excellent (often selfless) assistants but not very good businessmen and women on your own account.

You work better in company than singly. You are authors, singers, scientists, priests, politicians and poets. Orderly and well-disciplined workers, you are well respected. Albert Einstein and Copernicus were both Pisces.

Chapter 5

Money and How to Handle it

Any fool can get money, my father said once; it is holding on to it and accumulating it that is difficult.

Learn here how the stars may guide you about your strongest and weakest points in the handling of money, for *forewarned is forearmed*. It is not enough to love your work, it is also necessary to earn enough money to keep you in the comfortable state of life with which your labours should reward you. There is no shame or dishonour in making a profit from your own efforts, although in greed there is a conflict with conscience, and shame. *The labourer is worthy of his hire* (Luke, X. vii). So many people blame money and wealth for the evils of the world, when it is clear that money is wholly neutral; it never corrupts anybody in whom the seeds of moral decay were not available for growth.

By understanding our personal relationship to money, wealth and knowing how we handle it we can take steps to see that we do not use it badly, selfishly and cruelly.

To develop yourself to your highest potential try to understand all the advantages your star sign offer you; build upon this and you will find there is a solid foundation.

BUSINESS

Aries (21 March to 20 April)
Inclined to spend money in a big, openhanded way –

especially prone to wanting to make a big impression. Alone without emotional pressures or ill-timed advice from friends or experts you can succeed very well just by using your own shrewd intuition and natural cunning.

Taurus (21 April to 21 May)

You do not rush in sometimes with taurine tenacity where the angels might well tremble to tread. You are very materialistic, loving and needing money not for itself, but rather for what you can buy with it. You hold on to what you get. Do not become so obsessed by ideas and hopes that you ruin your financial position beyond repair.

Gemini (22 May to 20 June)

Alas! How much you do love money. It amuses you to reap the golden harvest. The extraordinary thing is that you give it away, spend it and waste it as if it were contaminated. You rank among the big-time spenders. Your quick wit and intelligence make it fairly easy for you to get money – you are very adaptable : you can and will work at anything. Never play cards or gamble for *big stakes* – it can ruin you.

Cancer (21 June to 22 July)

Your way of living is such that money is of scant importance. You are thrifty and can save for many things you want, but just as easily spend the lot in a burst of shopping. You like a gamble and are frequently lucky people, but must never spend all your time in gambling. Your luck runs in cycles – you cannot force it.

Leo (23 July to 22 August)

Probably the most materialist of all signs, you suffer more than any other sign from poverty. Money is the key to power, influence and mastery. It is the gateway to the luxury you crave. You love to be the openhanded host, to shower gifts and wealth upon those you love – even upon strangers at times! You will risk everything you have to get wealth – but have often no mental or moral reserves if you fail – as in Shakespeare's –

> *to fall like Lucifer*
> *never to hope again.*

Virgo (23 August to 22 September)

You are among the great economists of the world; you can pinch and save better than almost any other sign. You achieve miracles on a relatively small income. You are seldom gamblers and should avoid risking big sums. When you invest money you prefer solid investments with a lower, safe and sure interest. Your weakness is that if *convinced* that some scheme or plan is *safe* you may fall easily into difficulties.

Libra (23 September to 22 October)

You can be hardheaded, thorough businessmen and women, but are frequently quite daring and will take very heavy risks. Generosity is often overdone. To cheat a Libran is to invite a lifelong hatred: Librans are not noted for forgiveness. Librans are extremely clever with money, but often do not get sufficient opportunity to develop their talents.

Scorpio (23 October to 21 November)

You are fairly good businessmen and know how to use wealth to influence and control others. Frequently you become selfish and ruthless. In business and gambling you show a hardness which completely disguises your softer sentiments. You make the best roulette, bingo or poker players and professional bridge players.

Sagittarius (22 November to 20 December)

You either despise wealth or you worship it. You are gamblers and adventurers who will undergo terrible risks and hardships to get what you want. As long as you have a definite objective you can work magnificently for it. You are seldom down for long.

Capricorn (21 December to 19 January)
You are instinctive savers; you dislike any risk which has no *logical success* clearly in sight. You take little pride in what you hoard, but tend to work out expenditure to the very last penny. Often you are so busy reckoning expenditure that you are careless about increasing income : remember that!

Aquarius (20 January to 18 February)
Strange idealists! You value money mainly for what you can use it for – but you can be very versatile in handling money. You can take risks that very few other signs would ever take – and you frequently win. Unfortunately you sometimes try to force your ideas and ideals into your business life and suffer badly from it. You are too generous for your own welfare, but sometimes you learn in time and manage to make a comfortable life for yourself.

Pisces (19 February to 20 March)
To tell the truth, you just are *not* good businessmen or women. You are liable to be conned and tricked too easily. You rarely sense danger before it hits you. A gamble with small odds will serve you better than any heavy risks. All investments should be in solid securities.

Chapter 6

What are your Chances of becoming Famous?

How many of us dream of becoming famous? Many long to achieve something of note before we pass away.

What a wonderful opportunity for achievement life may become!

What are your chances of becoming remembered, honoured and treasured by the rest of Mankind?

Read from this list what spheres of human greatness are most commonly excelled in by those born under the same sign as yourself; examine yourself carefully, reflect upon the things you succeeded in best while at school, think what instinctive (if hitherto concealed) wishes you have had. Maybe you wanted to write an opera, construct a computer, sail round the world single-handed, climb a mountain, write a book, a film-script or a play, become a world-famous scientist.

See what the others in your birthsign have achieved and then try, try, try again.

Aries (21 March to 20 April)
Hans Christian *Andersen* – 2 April 1805
  Not only a writer of children's stories but a great philosopher.
Johann Sebastian *Bach* – 21 March 1685
  One of the world's greatest composers.

William *Booth* – 10 April 1829
  Reformer, Founder of Salvation Army.
Prince *Bismarck* – 1 April 1815
  Political genius and man of letters.
Lucretia *Borgia* – 18 April 1480
  Ruthless politician and famous beauty.

Charlie *Chaplin* – 16 April 1889
Comedian, actor and composer.

Anatole *France* – 16 April 1844
One of France's greatest writers, noted for gentle satire, very sympathetic and perceptive.

Francisco de *Goya* – 30 March 1746
Spain's most significant painter.

Joseph *Haydn* – 31 March 1732
Prolific composer of beautiful music.

Adolf *Hitler* – 20 April 1889
Reformer and ruthless politician.

Wilhelm *Röntgen* – 27 March 1845
Human benefactor. Discoverer of X rays.

Arturo *Toscanini* – 27 March 1867
Musician: one of the greatest conductors of his day.

Emile *Zola* – 2 April 1840.
Reformer and author.

Taurus (21 April to 21 May)

Honoré de *Balzac* – 20 May 1799
One of the world's great writers.

Johann *Brahms* – 7 May 1833
Great composer of symphonies, violin concerto, etc.

Oliver *Cromwell* – 25 April 1599
Deeply religious reformer, perceptive, sensitive, logical and artistic. Greatly maligned by his enemies. A brilliant military commander.

Alphonse *Daudet* – 13 May 1840
One of the world's great writers. Brilliant but gentle humorist.

F. *Fröbel* – 21 April 1782
Educational reformer.

Immanuel *Kant* – 22 April 1724
Philosopher who profoundly influenced his era.

Nicolo *Machiavelli* – 3 May 1469
Writer of exceptional ability and daring who chronicled satirically the political morality and trends of his day. He also wrote very fine poetry.

Karl *Marx* – 5 May 1818
German writer upon whose theories Russia built communism.

Florence *Nightingale* – 12 May 1870
Reformer and founder of organised nursing. A selfless worker for the sick and suffering.

Max *Planck* – 23 April 1858
Scientist.

Piotr *Tchaikovsky* – 7 May 1840
Composer of some of the world's greatest love music.

Gemini (22 May to 20 June)

Sir Arthur *Conan-Doyle* – 22 May 1859
Writer. Inventor of Sherlock Holmes.

Sir Anthony *Eden* – 12 June 1897
Diplomat. Brilliant linguist.

Paul *Gaughin* – 7 June 1848
Artist.

Edward *Grieg* – 15 June 1843
Lyrical composer with exceptional talent.

Carl *Linneus* – 23 May 1707
Brilliant scientist who established the scientific method of classifying plants. Benefactor to herbalist and botanists alike.

Thomas *Mann* – 6 June 1875
Profound author of outstanding ability.

Blaise *Pascal* – 19 June 1623
Writer and philosopher.

Robert *Schumann* – 8 June 1810
Composer.

Richard *Strauss* – 11 June 1864
Composer.

Rabinandrath *Tagore* – 7 June 1861
Poet and thinker of considerable talent.

Queen *Victoria* – 25 May 1819
Powerful personality who influenced both government policy and the social scene of her day.

Richard *Wagner* –
Germany's most powerful and dynamic composer; he wrote his own poetry for many of his operas.

Walt *Whitman* – 31 May 1819
America's treasured poet whose '*Leaves of Grass*' had a profound effect upon several generations.

Cancer (21 June – 22 July)

Roald *Amundsen* – 16 July 1872
Intrepid and famous explorer.

Pearl *Buck* – 26 June 1892
Writer with profound understanding of human problems and sorrow.

Calvin – 10 July 1509
Severe, puritanical religious reformer.

Giuseppe *Garibaldi* – 4 July 1807
Founder of modern Italy; fearless fighter and statesman.

Ernest *Hemingway* – 21 July 1898
Writer with deep comprehension of human conflict and contact.

Gottfried *Keller* – 19 July 1819
Switzerland's famous master of literature.

Trygve *Lie* – 16 July 1896
Great contributor to international understanding.

Gina *Lollobrigida* – 4 July 1928
Very talented actress.

Gustav *Mahler* – 7 July 1860
Lyricist and composer.

Jacques *Offenbach* – 21 June 1819
Operettist and composer.

Leo (23 July to 22 August)

Stanley *Baldwin* – 3 August 1867
English politician.

Simon *Bolivar* – 24 July 1783
Liberator, general and statesman.

Emily *Brontë* – 30 July 1818
Authoress, poetess; her 'Wuthering Heights' is an immortal classic.

Claude *Debussy* – 22 August 1802
Famous composer.

Alexandre *Dumas* – 24 July 1807
One of the world's greatest story-tellers.

Henry *Ford* – 30 July 1863
Developer of the motor car. His genius placed it in the reach of all income brackets.

John *Galsworthy* – 14 August 1867
Famous author.

Carl Gustav *Jung* – 26 July 1875
Psychologist.

Mata *Hari* – 7 August 1876
Dancer and spy.

Benito *Mussolini* – 29 July 1883
Italian reformer and politician.

Napoleon Bonaparte – 15 August 1769
French general and politician.

George Bernard *Shaw* – 26 July 1856
Dramatist and literary critic.

Virgo (23 August to 22 September)

Jean Louis *Barrault* – 8 September 1910
Actor and artist.

Ingrid *Bergman* – 29 August 1917
Actress.

Michael *Faraday* – 22 September 1791
Famous scientist.

Greta *Garbo* – 18 September 1905
Exceptionally brilliant actress.

Johann Wolfgang *Goethe* – 28 August 1749
One of the greatest dramatists, poets and authors the world has ever known.

Maurice *Maeterlinck* – 29 August 1862
The exceptional poet and dramatist of Belgium.

Girolamo *Savonarola* – 21 September 1452
Courageous religious and political reformer.

Leo *Tolstoy* – 9 September 1828
Author and reformer.

H. G. *Wells* – 21 September 1866
Gifted author and scientist, many of whose prophecies have come to pass.

Libra (23 September to 22 October)

Henri *Bergson* – 18 October 1859
Philosopher.

Annie *Besant* – 1 October 1847
Political and religious reformer.

Antonio *Canaletto* – 8 October 1697
Remarkably talented painter.

Eleonore *Duse* – 3 October 1859
Talented actress of legendary ability.

J. D. *Eisenhower* – 14 October 1890
Renowned general and politician.

Mahatma *Gandhi* – 2 October 1869
Lawyer, religious and political leader.

Rita *Hayworth* – 17 October 1918
Attractive, talented actress.

M. *Le Corbusier* – 6 October 1887
Greatly-admired architect.

Alfred *Nobel* – 21 October 1833
Inventor of dynamite, and donor of the Nobel prize foundation.

G. *Verdi* – 10 October 1813
Composer whose operas are internationally treasured by music lovers.

Oscar *Wilde* – 15 October 1856
Witty, homosexual dramatist and poet.

Scorpio (23 October to 21 November)

St. *Augustine* – 13 November 354
Churchman and missionary.

Georges *Bizet* – 25 October 1838
Composer of lively and popular music.

Albert *Camus* – 7 November 1913
Writer and thinker.

Georges *Danton* – 28 October 1759
Political fanatic.

F. *Engels* – 28 November 1820
Political theorist.

Erasmus – 28 October 1465
Religious reformer.

William *Hogarth* – 10 November 1697
Famous satirical painter.

Selma *Lagerlöf* – 20 November 1858
One of Sweden's greatest writers.

Martin *Luther* – 10 October 1483
One of the world's most significant religious reformers.

I. *Nehru* – 14 November 1889
India's liberator and politician.

Pablo *Picasso* – 23 October 1881
Artist.

Leon *Trotsky* – 7 November 1879
Political theorist.

Ivan *Turganev* – 9 November 1818
Great writer of short stories.

Voltaire – 21 November 1694
Brilliant satirist.

Sagittarius (22 November to 20 December)

L. van *Beethoven* – 17 December 1770
World-famous composer.

William *Blake* – 28 November 1757
Seer and poet.

Sir Winston *Churchill* – 30 November 1874
Adventurer, journalist and statesman who achieved world renown.

Josef *Conrad* – 6 December 1857
Writer of wonderful sea stories etc.

Walt *Disney* – 5 December 1901
Few men have brought so much happiness to so many children. Cartoonist.

Charles *de Gaulle* – 22 November 1890
France's politician and general.

Heinrich *Heine* – 13 December 1797
Satirical and lyrical poet.

Jean *Sibelius* – 8 December 1865
One of the world's most gifted composers – and tone poets.

Werner *Siemens* – 13 December 1816
Scientist who founded an electrical industry.

Mark *Twain* – 30 November 1835
He founded a whole tradition of humorous writing.

Stefan *Zweig* – 28 November 1881
Famous author.

Capricorn (21 December to 19 January)

Konrad *Adenauer* – 5 January 1876

One of Germany's cleverest statesmen.

Clement *Attlee* – 3 January 1883
Socialist politician.

Paul *Cezanne* – 19 January 1839
Talented artist.

Marlene *Dietrich* – 27 December 1904
Internationally-applauded actress.

Benjamin *Franklin* – 17 January 1706
Philosopher, scientist and statesman.

Rudyard *Kipling* – 30 December 1865
Author and poet with unrivalled understanding of human nature.

Henri *Matisse* – 31 December 1869
Famous artist.

C. L. *Montesquieu* – 18 January 1689
Brilliant journalist and profound philosopher.

Jean *Racine* – 21 December 1639
One of France's most revered poets and dramatists.

Albert *Schweitzer* – 14 January 1875
Doctor of Music, Doctor of Philosophy, Doctor of Medicine; One of the greatest organists of all times. He forsook all honours and glory to tend the sick in a primitive hospital at Lambarene in the then French West Africa.

Woodrow *Wilson* – 28 December 1856
Lofty idealist and politician, one of the founders of the League of Nations.

Aquarius (20 January to 18 February)

A. *Adler* – 7 February 1870

One of the most logical psychologists.

Karl M. *Bellman* – 4 February 1740
One of Sweden's greatest lyric poets.

Lord *Byron* – 22 January 1788
Adventurer and sensuous poet of great talent. He died helping the Greeks free themselves from the Turks, and is honoured in Greece.

S. *Colette* – 28 January 1873
Prolific French writer of love stories.

Charles *Darwin* – 12 February 1809
Assiduous scientist of marked ability.

Thomas A. *Edison* – 11 February 1847
The most versatile and beneficial scientist and inventor the world has ever known.

Frederick the Great – 24 January 1712
King of Prussia, founder of Prussian military and industrial power.

Clark *Gable* – 1 February 1901
Romantic actor.

Ernest *Haeckel* – 16 February 1834
Very independent philosopher and zoologist.

G. *Lessing* – 22 January 1729
Writer, poet, critic, dramatist, champion of religious tolerance.

Abraham *Lincoln* – 12 February 1809
Idealist, lawyer, politician and champion of anti-slavery.

Charles *Lindbergh* – 4 February 1902
Hero of first New York to Paris non-stop flight.

General *MacArthur* – 26 January 1880
One of America's greatest military commanders.

Somerset *Maugham* – 25 January 1874
Doctor. Author of exceptional talent and perception. Former intelligence agent.

Felix *Mendelssohn* – 3 February 1809
Few composers' music have created so much happiness.

Wolfgang Amadeus *Mozart* – 25 January 1756
Unrivalled composer of symphonies who developed from infant prodigy to genius.

F. D. *Roosevelt* – 30 January 1882
American politician and reformer.

Paul Henri *Spaak* – 25 January 1899
Politician and one of the founding fathers of the united Europe movement.

Jules *Verne* – 8 February 1828
Fabulously inventive writer, father of science fiction, popular for over a century.

Pisces (19 February to 20 March)

Gabriele *d'Annunzio* – 12 March 1863
Poet, whose works are full of beauty, and soldier.

Chopin 22 February 1810
World-famed romantic composer.

Benedetto *Croce* – 25 February 1868
Renowned philosopher.

Albert *Einstein* – 14 March 1879
Mathematician and philosopher.

Beniamo *Gigli* – 20 March 1890
Tenor whose voice gave joy to millions.

Victor *Hugo* – 26 February 1802

One of France's most unforgettable authors.

Henrik *Ibsen* – 20 March 1828
Norway's exceptionally brilliant dramatist, poet and social reformer.

David *Livingstone* – 19 March 1813
Famous missionary and explorer of Africa.

Thomas *Masaryk* – 7 March 1850
Statesman, father of Czechoslovakia.

Karl *May* – 25 February 1842
Germany's favourite author for boys of all ages from 8 to 80.

Michelangelo – 6 March 1475
Sculptor of world renown.

Nicolai *Rimski Korsakov* – 18 March 1844
Composer.

George *Washington* – 22 February 1732
General, statesman, father of the United States of America.

Chapter 7

What you wear reveals your Personality and affects your Fate and Fortune

The Swiss author Gottfried Keller wrote a very amusing story about a poor, unsuccessful tailor who donned some truly elegant clothes designed for a rich man and was accepted as a foreign nobleman by Society . . . and as such made his fortune. '*Clothes are the Making of People*' is not only a novel, it is one of the facts of life.

Have you ever dreamed that your birthsign is closely linked with the sort of things you wear? That fashions are applicable only to people within certain Zodiac groupings? How is it that an actress or actor who may look the spit and image of you can wear some clothes which are quite identical to those for which you paid the same money, but still look better than you do? Simple, you are following somebody else's birthsign. He or she may be Taurus for example, and you may be Sagittarius . . . your fashions must be for you alone. There are limits as to what any one birthsign can wear . . . how well do you know how to make the best of your appearance? Do you really know what to wear to make the best impression?

An Aquarian can wear what an Aries subject could never wear without looking sloppy.

Study this section carefully; by understanding what is written here you will stand a better chance of making a better impression next time you wish to get the best out of your clothing, and, male or female, you can save yourself a lot at the sales, by learning whether to adopt a popular fashion or not. Do not forget that some fashions may be the very opposite of what it is advisable for you to wear.

STYLES

Aries (21 March to 20 April)

If in doubt use suits of grey or occasionally darker shades. Avoid scarlet, pillarbox red, vermilion, but orange is all right. You wear almost any shades of green elegantly. You should use violently strong colours sparingly. Some Aries have talent in designing their own clothes and look very chic in them.

Taurus (21 April to 21 May)

You are very clothes-conscious and very easily depressed if you have to wear old or dirty garments. You appreciate well-cut clothes very much. Generally your taste tends to the elegant and chic – seldom does the bizarre attract you. Thin stripes appeal to you but if you are portly avoid horizontal lines which could emphasise any surplus flesh! Taurus people like all their clothes to be comfortable to live in – however expensive. Blue shades, light greens and pale oranges are good for you to wear.

Gemini (22 May to 20 June)

You are often so indifferent to clothes as to be almost unaware whether you are clothed or not. You prefer practical, useful clothing, hardwearing, with pockets, Harris tweeds perhaps, faded jeans; the extraordinary thing is that you wear almost anything with grace, charm and elegance which enhance your personality. The secret is that you love to keep yourself spotlessly clean. All-black should not be worn, only one thing now and then black. Most colours suit you.

Cancer (21 June to 22 July)
Pastel blues, greens and some shades of brown are very popular among Cancer subjects. Usually, you like clothes which are comfortable; yes, you like elegance indeed, but it is comfort you tend to put first. Cancer people are often at their best in clothes which fit their bodies – thin clothing (weather permitting). Generally-speaking, large, floppy clothing is wrong for Cancer people.

Leo (23 July to 22 August)
Alas! Clothing is one of your marked weaknesses, few signs of the Zodiac spend so much on their wardrobe as do Leos! You like strong positive colours and seldom look your best in pale or pastel colours. Try to moderate your chic by good taste; to be smart is quite different to being bizarre or loud. Do not trust the advice of sales assistants when they ' recommend ' something to you. You have a weakness for very elaborate jewellery and ornaments.

Virgos (23 August to 22 September)
How you love to be smart, well dressed, chic and in the topline of fashion! You have a remarkable ability to look smart in very simple (even old) clothing. Most of you can design new, alter or re-touch old clothing for yourselves. You enjoy fashions and follow them quite eagerly. It is neither possible to make general recommendations nor necessary, because Virgos have from an early age very good instincts as to what they should wear.

Libra (23 September to 22 October)
Your taste is usually impeccable – certainly it is limited only by your purse (or wallet). You can wear rags and look like a duke or a duchess. One tip – keep to light, well-balanced colours. Few people are so well able to blend simple things and make old things look like Paris or Savile Row. It is just as well, for Librans suffer terribly from the

pettiness and jealousy of others and are often poor as a result. Only Aquarians are not jealous of you but, fascinating as they are, you never trust them wholly.

Scorpio (23 October to 21 November)
What peculiar extremes Scorpios display! You can be the sloppiest dressers or the very height of fashion! You like to be valued for yourself alone, and sometimes dress to shock or stun your neighbours as much as to fulfil your own needs. Few signs of the Zodiac are so smart in screaming reds as are Scorpio subjects.

Sagittarius (22 November to 20 December)
You look your best, most attractive and happiest, in sportswear and informal clothing. Blues and whites are good colours for most Sagittarians.

Capricorn (21 December to 19 January)
Your sign is one which gives you most elegance in dark colours; but the truth of the matter is that you are one of the least clothes-conscious people of the entire Zodiac. Find out which clothes make you most elegant : keep the styles that suit you – avoid fashions, they are seldom created with you in mind.

Aquarius (20 January to 18 February)
For the average Aquarian, clothes are a delight, a toy but not a necessity. You achieve a certain INSOUCIANCE, an attractive, raffish charm in almost anything. You are extremely daring, innovators of fashion, but can show delicacy and taste in dress to rank with the very leaders of elegance and fashion. Your clothes are (within your financial limits) a total projection of yourself – as you want others to see you. Few signs can use clothes to express their sexuality as do Aquarians – almost by accident, usually there is restraint to avoid flamboyance.

Pisces (19 February to 20 March)

You prefer comfort to fashion, you will hang on to old comfy clothes and slippers long after they should have been bestowed on a museum. Strange to say, your preferred, sloppy, favourite clothes often make you look comfortable and cuddly: other signs would never get away with such a thing. Wear what you like instinctively: you'll look your best in that.

F

Chapter 8

Sports

As the Ancient Greeks well knew, life is not just intended to be one dreary round of drudgery; Man is intended to relax, to enjoy the happy things that life can offer.

Many are the sports and activities which open up to us the possibilities within ourselves, develop our characters, but only a few of them can give us the success which is the crowning glory, the key to satisfaction, so it is important for you to see which of them are most likely to give you a fair chance.

If you like a sport which is not listed under your sign it does not mean you cannot make a success of it, but it might well and truly pay you to try those suggested under the appropriate signs.

So many people have, in their schooldays and youth, a chance to try only one or two sports, often neither of which is suitable. Many a champion may be waiting to be discovered.

Success in sport is so often the very first clue to the energy, self-discipline, power and determination which lie in wait in each of us, and it needs this to bring it out into the open.

Not only is there all the possibility of your developing yourself, but also the certainty that life will give you more fun, new friends, new opportunities.

Aries (21 March to 20 April)
You need contact with nature to enjoy good health. Athletics, combat sports (boxing, judo, karate, wrestling), motor car and cycle racing, rambling for older subjects. Baseball, football, cricket, also appeal.

Taurus (21 April to 21 May)
For you, gymnastics, running and swimming are indicated. Ballroom dancing and iceskating are also attractive.

Gemini (22 May to 20 June)
Although not all Gemini people like sport, some excel at light athletics, springboard diving etc. Bridge and chess are very attractive to you.

Cancer (21 June to 22 July)
Team sports will not usually appeal to you, but a long run through the woods in a tracksuit, a trip across heath and moorlands with a rucksack, a good swim, are much enjoyed. You will love camping and adventure journeys into the wilds, canoe trips and pony trekking, and lone sailing (just one or two aboard).

Leo (23 July to 22 August)
You love hard, competitive sports :– rugger, soccer, hockey, combat sports, but prefer sports in which you can lead. Golf is popular among older Leos.

Virgo (23 August to 22 September)
You are *not* among the most boisterous sportsmen of the world, but yachting, ski-ing (especially apres ski parties) will appeal to you. Can do well in ballet and enrhythmics.

Libra (23 September to 22 October)
Diving (highboard and springboard), swimming, skating (ice and roller), dancing, gymnastics, tennis and ski-ing are for you.

Scorpio (23 October to 21 November)
Archery, fishing, hunting, shooting, mountaineering, anything adventurous and daring fascinates you.

Sagittarius (22 November to 20 December)
Archery, shooting, racing in any form, motoring, flying, climbing, rambling, show-jumping, horse-riding, skindiving. The more exciting the sport the greater is your fun.

Capricorn (21 December to 19 January)
Not a very sportive sign, but capable of good results in climbing, walking, rambling, weight-lifting etc.

Aquarius (20 January to 18 February)
Either not interested or extreme enthusiasts – the Aquarians can excel at any sport or games that take their fancy. Individual rather than team sports are best. Aquarians can show great moral fibre and toughness. Agility, speed and endurance come naturally to them but not too easily.

Pisces (19 February to 20 March)
Swimming, sailing, fishing and powerboat sailing appeal to you.

Chapter 9

How a Horoscope is drawn up

The way in which a professional astrologer draws up
a horoscope is very much more complicated than the
simple predictions in a paper or magazine lead us to
expect.

It is not just a matter of calculating which day of the
period one is born upon, but also the hour, so that the
influences of planets and so on can be estimated.

SUN POSITION
The position of the Sun, relative to the time of day, is
important because it is held to represent the ability to
express your personality throughout your life, the amount
of physical and mental vitality. Dividing the 12 hours of
daylight into groups of three fours, it is possible for any
amateur to estimate the significance of ascendance, zenith,
and waning throughout the day.

On charts with traditional drawings the East is shown
on the left.

THE MOON
Represents feminine or negative rhythms and as such is
indicative of the habits, mannerisms and behavioural patterns to be expected – how much the person follows the
traditional tendencies of his star.

And so we come to the planets, each of which is said to

affect the strength of the influence of the birthsign within certain directions.

The planets are also said to affect a reading, and are spoken of as follows: Planet . . . in the . . . house.

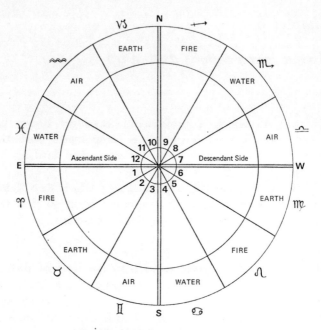

i) The thick N–S and E–W lines are called MAIN CUSPS
ii) The numbered areas are called HOUSES
The lines between them are called CUSPS
iii) The zodiac sign along the E–W line varies with each horoscope.

ASCENDANTS

Whichever sign was rising in the East at the time of your birth is drawn in the East of the chart, and is said to be in the ascendant.

The sign which is rising is very important and the following influences are to be expected:–

Aries: You will be a go-getter, positive and more demanding than is usual, even for Aries. Most of your desires can be obtained by discipline and a high degree of moral and physical courage.

Taurus: This brings a stabilising influence, ability to assume responsibilities, dependability – all you need is the determination to work hard for the goals you consider should be yours.

Gemini: A large share of the world's riches can be yours; travel will help you achieve your aims; you must work hard to develop your powers of concentration.

Cancer: As with no other ascendant, women will bring you luck; they are linked to your economic progress. Friendships are vitally important to your success. You must fight laziness and wanderlust.

Leo: Few can achieve the magnificent heights of success so well as when Leo is rising in their horoscope. Regardless of sex, your greatest help will come from men. When you take advice be careful that you know the friend who gives it.

Virgo: Your strong point will be ability to accept duties, to plod along with hard work and routine which others without this ascendant cannot easily endure. You must speak up for yourself to get a fair deal.

Libra: Your great need is to work with others, to work in harness however you may feel that you outrank them. Use your heart as well as your intelligence to make for success. Study human nature to understand people fully.

Scorpio: This sign ascendant increases the power of your intuition and the depth of your affections. You must guard against the sacrifice of your life ambitions to the domination of others.

Sagittarius: Provided that you work conscientiously for your plans you will find a Midas touch attending your efforts. Your greatest weaknesses are yourself, and an occasional sense of inertia.

Capricorn: When this planet is rising you will most likely achieve your greatest success and happiness later in life. Endurance and patience are strong points.

Aquarius:　You have a wonderful gift for friendship, and make much success through this. Your greatest weakness lies in a tendency to try to do too many things at one and the same time. Versatile, you can master one field at a time.

Pisces:　Your strength will be in using sympathy and subtlety to achieve success. You will have a gift for tolerance and genuine selflessness.

NOT ONLY TIME BUT PLACE

Every place in the world is said to have an affinity to some constellation or other of the Zodiac, and it may be totally impossible for you to achieve success if you live in an area whose sign negates the positive good your own sign can offer you.

Such details involve a very great deal of mathematical precision, the use of complicated tables and so on.

Other influences

In the chart the number of planets which occupy Air and Fire houses indicate the amount of positiveness the person can muster.

The element group (Air, etc) which contains most planetary influences will be the strongest influence in your life.

STARS AND HERBS OF HEALING

One of the oldest unbroken traditions in the world is that of herbal treatment in times of sickness. The true herbalist does not accept completely the methods of classifying illnesses, diagnosis or treatment that are used by the established medical authorities. Herbal treatments are remarkably successful and are noted for not having the side-effects for which many of the modern man-made drugs are infamous. Some observations have been made over the centuries, and it seems that persons under certain birthsigns

of the Zodiac often react best when treated with herbs
which are considered to be under their sign.

Aries: Broom tops, garlic, hops, and nettle tops.

Taurus: Coltsfoot, sage, tansy, thyme, uva-ursi.

Gemini: Caraway seeds, meadowsweet, parsley and the
following which should only be used under directions
of a herbalist – lily of the valley and skullcap: these
herbs are not dangerous, but doses required vary
according to patient's age and condition, a direction
for this sign only.

Cancer: Chickweed, honeysuckle, lettuce.

Leo: Eyebright, marigold flowers, mistletoe (under
herbalist's direction only), St. John's wort, and walnut.

Virgo: Fennel, liquorice, skullcap.

Libra: Archangel, catmint, feverfew, pennyroyal, thyme
and violets.

Scorpio: Blackberries, carduus benedictus, horseradish,
leeks.

Sagittarius: Agrimony, burdock, clover (red), and dande-
lions.

Capricorn: Comfreyroots, fumitory, equisetum arvense,
slippery elm and thyme.

Aquarius: Comfrey, nettles, marigolds, snake root, slippery elm, tansy.

Pisces: Burnet saxifrage, camomile, carrageen moss,
Lungwort, Poplar bark, Peppermint, Verbena.

For details about herbs, how to collect them, dry, use and
what doses to give, and for which illnesses to give them,
consult any of these books by me :–

Concise Herbal Encyclopaedia
                        (Published by Bartholomew)
Herbgrowing for Health   (Published by John Gifford)
Herbal Teas for Health and Pleasure
                        (Health Science Press)

JEWELS

It has been a tradition of astrologers throughout history that certain jewels carry radiations which are in themselves, and in their colours, fortunate, or bringers of luck (in that they seem to enhance the positiveness of the person of that birthsign carrying them in any form).

The following seem to be widely agreed upon, and it will be interesting to see how much they can assist you in achieving positiveness and success.

Aries :	Ruby, jasper (red), or sardonyx.
Taurus :	Emerald, malachite, or carnelian.
Gemini :	Diamond, onyx, agate.
Cancer :	Turquoise, green beryl, green jasper.
Leo :	Topaz, zircon, yellow stones.
Virgo :	Chrysoberyl, emerald, possibly green jade.
Libra :	Jade (green).
Scorpio :	Carnelian, bloodstone.
Sagittarius :	Sapphire or pink quartz.
Capricorn :	Serpentine (ophite), possibly black opals.
Aquarius :	One of the most authenticated of all birthstones; nearly all sources, however far apart, indicate that the amethyst is almost sacred to Aquarians; some sources recommend sapphire or aquamarine.
Pisces :	Opal or jasper.

PLANETS AND ASSOCIATED INFLUENCES

Planet	*Lucky Colour*	*Lucky Metal*
Mars	Orange	Iron
Venus	Red	Copper
Mercury	Green	Mercury (Quicksilver)
Sun	Blue	Gold
Moon	White	Silver
Saturn	Yellow	Lead
Jupiter	Purple	Tin

SIGNS OF THE ZODIAC AND SHORTAGES OF MINERAL SALTS
IN THE BLOOD

Some American research has postulated that certain birth-signs show a predisposition to run short of specific mineral salts more than other groups, and indicates that if illnesses, malaise, or depression sets in the person should immediately take some plant or other substance which contains these salts.

Aries :	Potassium phosphate
Taurus :	Sodium sulphate
Gemini :	Potassium chloride
Cancer :	Calcium fluoride
Leo :	Magnesium phosphate
Virgo :	Potassium sulphate
Libra :	Sodium phosphate
Scorpio :	Calcium sulphate
Sagittarius :	Silica
Capricorn :	Calcium phosphate
Aquarius :	Sodium chloride
Pisces :	Ferrous phosphate

N.B. Many pharmaceutists supply these, as do health stores, in the form of readily prepared bio-chemic salts, made up according to the formulae of Dr H. Schüssler the great homoeopathic physician.

Chapter 10

Palmistry - a Do-It-Yourself Guide

The knowledge of palmistry goes back beyond the musty records of history. Certainly in India it has been practised for thousands of years, and it is still widely used there.

I think the one point I would like to make is that the lines on hands and so forth indicate the trends of destiny. There is no proof that our destiny is *written*, a simple *kismet* from which there is no escape. Evidence shows that guide lines and warnings are available, but the ultimate choice is ours.

It has been found that some of the symptoms of diseases show up in hands and finger nails, I have given only two simple examples, because a layman's diagnosis may omit several other confirmatory or cancellatory details and cause more worry and fright than is justified.

This is by no means an alternative to visiting a really professional palmist. It is an explanation of the sort of things that a professional has to study. Naturally there are many other small lines, details, spots, bars, grilles, islands and so on to be found on the human palm but years of study are needed to interpret them.

This section of the book will enable you to read interesting, intimate and helpful details from people's hands. Many secrets, vital information about suitability for marriage and business potential are all here for you to read.

Everything has been simplified as far as possible. Some

authors describe things quite differently, but wherever possible I have used words and terminology that simplify the learning processes.

Some Indian palmists and others can make predictions of a fantastic nature from palms, but we must bear in mind many of them have a well developed Ring of Sibyl . . . the ancient wise woman so well known in Roman history, and as such their occult powers hinge upon clairvoyancy.

The profound and profuse amount of details available lead one to ponder whether there were at some time highly organised, scientists who codified all of these details, but whose work was lost in some deluge, cataclysm or global disaster.

The gypsies, whose language relates back to Ancient Sanskrit, brought the science with them from India, but it is widely practised throughout the world.

The Life Line.
The nearer the thumbside it starts the greater your intellectual power. If crisscrossed at the beginning early years will be crossed with illnesses. If it starts on Jupiter ambition will know no bounds. Several breaks in the middle denote financial hardships. Length of the Life line does not signify a short life; the line indicates problems of life, etc. A line starting from Venus and not the middle of the side of the hand denotes difficulty in ever settling down with one sexual partner. Branches leading from this line indicate tendency to dissipate strength and waste energies. If it sweeps out across the plain of Mars you have mental and physical toughness. If the line forks at its end you will tend to be footloose, love travel, and find it hard to settle down. If it ends on Diana emigration is fairly certain.

Line of Saturn.
Starts at the Bracelets, moves towards Mount Saturn. Deeply marked it promises financial prosperity. Broken lines indicate financial difficulties. If it ends at the Heart line

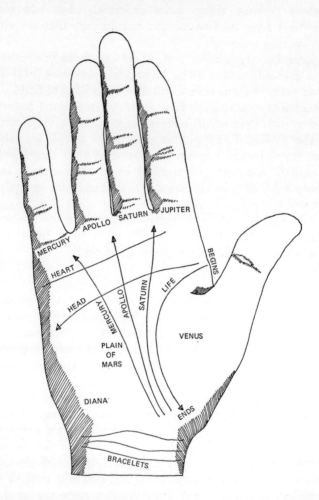

emotional affairs will get in the way of financial progress. If it breaks off at the Head line your intellectual interests will prevent you becoming really wealthy. If it leads to Jupiter your ambitions will succeed in making you rich. If to Apollo your money will be made through some art form.

Line of Apollo.
Starts at the bracelets, goes to Mount Apollo. Deeply marked, it indicates intellectual brilliancy, and your wealth and fame will come from purely intellectual, creative and artistic pursuits. If broken, your work will be spasmodic but not less successful. If it sweeps to Saturn you will tend to use your talents more for money than for art. If there is a gap where it crosses Heart and Head lines your emotional and/or intellectual pursuits may distract you from earning money.

Line of Mercury.
Starts at the bracelets, moves towards Mount Mercury. Deeply marked it implies your wealth and fame will come from pursuit of a learned profession. Gaps at the Heart and Head lines denote distractions which hinder your career.

The Bracelets.
Some palmists say that each circle represents either 25 or 30 years of life. If the top bracelet ascends into the plain of Mars you have strong sexual passions. If deeply marked, you have a strong hold on life. Good resistance to illnesses.

Head Line.
Starts in the same place as the Life line. It crosses over the hand to opposite side. Closely joined to Life line it shows lack of self-confidence in earlier years. If it drops downwards to Diana your emotions can interfere with your good judgment. If the end curls upwards towards Mount Mercury you have exceptional business acumen. If it is parallel to the Bracelets you are prosaic, extremely practical. Often the ending is forked, one end pointing up the other down. Downward sweeping line strengthens all literary and artistic talents. A thin Head line indicates narrowmindedness. A broad Head line shows an open, generous

mind. Deeply marked shows powerful concentration. Lightly marked indicates poor concentration. A narrow gap between Head and Heart line is a sign of more care needed in health matters. A wide gap indicates an extrovert, strong and healthy.

Heart Line.

Rises on or just below Mount Jupiter. If deeply marked and sweeping right across to Mount Diana the emotional side of your life is complicated by powerful sexual urges. If Diana is prominent you may suffer from envy – when the Heart line is strongly marked. If the beginning is forked you will tend to fall deeply in love, and trust too soon those who may not always reward your trust. If the line ends on Diana you are very sensuous and attractive to the opposite sex. If it curls upwards to Mercury you tend to demand too much of your partner. If the line has breaks or chainstitches you are flirtatious.

The Mounts of the Hand

Just behind the knuckles where the fingers join the hands, below the lines of the joins, there are one or two prominences visible on each hand. It is almost unknown for all four to be prominent. If one mount predominates these qualities will be most easily discernible in a person's temperament. If two predominate a personality will show some characteristics of both. The larger size (predominance) of a mount is easily visible to any untrained eye. From the left side (smallest finger) of the right hand going to the right the mounts are :–

Mercury.

Related to your capacity for achievement within almost every sphere of activity. Large and well rounded it denotes brilliance, quick-witted replies, a smooth-tongued person with the gift of the gab. Usually optimistic. Lithe and agile of body, athletic rather than massive.

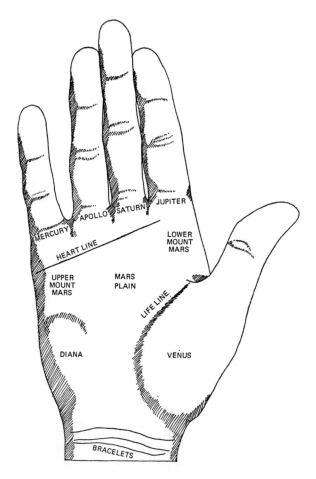

Apollo.
Large and well-rounded it betokens vivacity, strength, artistic talents and considerable originality of thought. If very large the person may have talent all right, but lack the practical sense to put it to good uses – such geniuses often die of hunger in a garret while posthumously their works fetch thousands.

G

Saturn.
Large and well rounded it signifies a solid, serious approach
to life. Very earnest, ability to plod along with tasks however dull. If other signs agree there is capacity for success
in very serious art forms (nothing new or changing).
Extremely large developments usually remain single unless
the Marriage line is strongly marked. Capacity for working
and living alone. Usually unemotional.

Jupiter.
A source of ambition. If very large it indicates ruthlessness
with self and other people. A tendency to dominate and
rule people and situations is marked when the mount is wel-
rounded and big. A sign of tremendous driving power and
needful for all go-getters.

Now Beneath the Heart Line.
From left to right . . .

Upper Mount Mars.
The larger this is so may you measure your combative-
ness, your will to resist, your capacity to fight, to lead, to
govern.

The Plain of Mars.
Strictly speaking this is not a mount. But we must deal with
it under this heading. It is the centre piece between the two
Mounts of Mars. If it is pleasantly curved inwards you
have a fairly even temper, if it is flattish and square in
shape there is too much hot-headedness, a tendency to rush
in where angels might fear to tread. Very deep hollowed
plains indicate a lack of resistance, lack of courage, weak-
willed personality.

Lower Mount Mars.
A measure of your physical strength ability to endure, to

hold on, to be patient. Its absence denotes inability to fight or endure.

Beneath the Line of the Head.
From left to right.

Mount Diana.
A large development is a measure of sympathy, warmth, interest in other people and other things. Harmony in all things. The mount should be firm. If it is soft, weak or flabby the affections will show as slobbery sentimentality and over-indulgence in emotions which are shallow.

Mount Venus.
This is basically the thumb side of the Life line. If it is flattish the person will be hard, unfeeling, indifferent to others. It is connoted to love, but more to family and marital love relationships (Diana is less discriminatory). It is also related to firmness of character, reliability and firmness of willpower. This is usually seen in how firm the flesh of the Mount is.

The Offside Edge of the Hand.
From the Bracelets going upwards.

Mount Neptune.
When this is large, firm, and rounded outwards there is a preference for holidays by the sea, by lake, canal side, sea travel, boats, canoes, yachts, fishing, etc.

Travel Forks.
Forked lines leading from Neptune are said to be connected with travel, and the more there are the more you will travel.

Family Line.
Just below the line of the Heart there is a line coming onto the Upper Mount Mars, and if this is deeply marked and

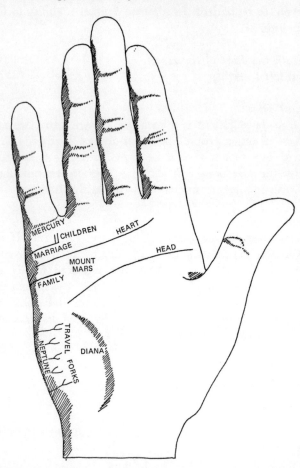

very clear so family life will play a great part in your life's happiness.

Marriage Line.
From the side coming onto the middle of Mount Mercury is the Marriage line; if absent you will probably stay single. If there are lines going upwards over Mount Mercury these represent the number of children you are likely to have.

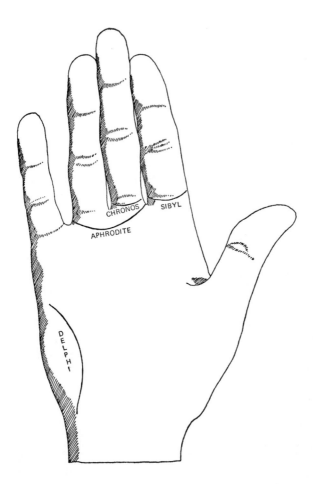

The Four Rings.

Delphi.
From Mt. Neptune across Mt. Diana. This endows you
with telepathic powers, awareness, shrewdness, and intuitive
powers which are rarely wrong.

Aphrodite.

Ends either on Mt. Apollo or Mt. Mercury, or between the two, takes its origin between Mt. Saturn and Mt. Jupiter. A fatal sign; sensual love and the desire to give yourselves to others and to take others to yourself will be a dominating streak of your nature. It is not related to affections or love or marriage.

Chronos.

According to its depth and clearness it will make you aware of the passage of Time, the need to accomplish things in life; if very large it may lead to introspection and despair at the speedy passing of the years.

Sibyl.

This is the occult sign. You will never be a master of occult sciences unless this ring is deeply marked on your finger base across the Mt. Jupiter. It endows you with a wise perception of the mysteries of life, facilitates a quick mastery of such things as telepathy, means you can master radiesthesia techniques and so on very quickly. You will make a good reader of palms, horoscopes; phrenologist, crystal gazer etc.

PECULIARITIES SEEN ON THE HANDS

SIGN	POSITION	MEANING
STAR	Mt. Apollo	Sudden access to money.
	Mt. Jupiter	Likelihood of legacy or gambling success.
	Mt. Mercury	Likely to marry rich woman/man.
CROSS	Mt. Venus	Ideal love match.
	Other mounts	Frustration for part of life of ideas connected with that mount.

PECULIARITIES SEEN ON THE HANDS

SQUARE	Any position	You will get out of difficulties connected with the mount or line by the skin of your teeth. Protection surrounds you.
TRIANGLE	Any position	Sudden change of luck for the better.
CIRCLE	On Neptune	Your life is in danger when you travel by water.
	Elsewhere	Danger connected with the ideas of the area on which it appears. Such danger is not usually lifelong.
ARROW	Anywhere	Beneficial influence affecting your life in relationship to the area where it strikes, i.e. your Head line with an arrow might mean success in invention, selling ideas etc.

WHAT THE APPEARANCE OF THE LINES MEANS

To be markedly effective a line should be visibly deep and slightly reddish in colour.

A straight line means no complications.

A line which looks like the chainstitches of knitting shows problems, often connected with health disorders.

A line which is undulating, showing distinct waves, shows indecision holding you back from achievements. This can be cured.

A reinforced line means strong help will come to help you in your achievements.

A line which is split up into segments denotes that you often lose out in the field of activity where they occur because you scatter your energies too widely and do not stick firmly enough to your intentions.

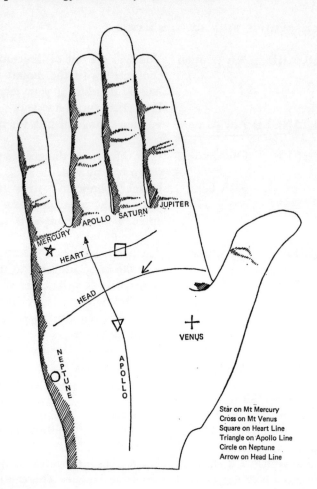

Star on Mt Mercury
Cross on Mt Venus
Square on Heart Line
Triangle on Apollo Line
Circle on Neptune
Arrow on Head Line

FINGERS AND THUMBS

When you read a hand ask the subject to clench the fist and suddenly open it. Note which of the fingers naturally spring upwards, and which just lie down slackly. The fingers are governed by the Mounts at their bases, and this shows you at once the dominant personality traits.

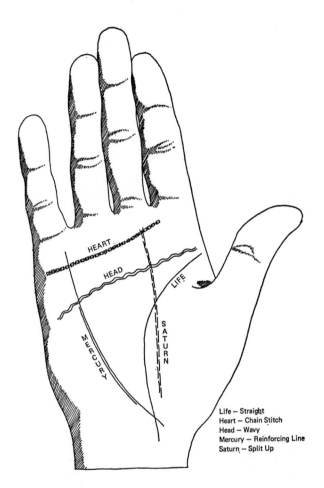

Life — Straight
Heart — Chain Stitch
Head — Wavy
Mercury — Reinforcing Line
Saturn — Split Up

Length of Fingers.
If the second finger can bend over and reach the bracelets it is a long finger. If it only reaches the Life line it is a medium finger; if not so far it is a short finger.

Shape.
Fingers are pointed, square, blunt or round at their ends.

Thumbs.

Either thick or thin. Long or short. Note angle at which they lie open from the fingers.

Hands.

There are two basic forms – the Square and the Hand of the Invisible Apex (because the lines of 1st. and 4th. fingers would meet at an apex if their lines were extended). Everything else is a variation of these.

REFER TO THE FOLLOWING CHARTS FOR
EXPLANATION OF THE ABOVE DATA.

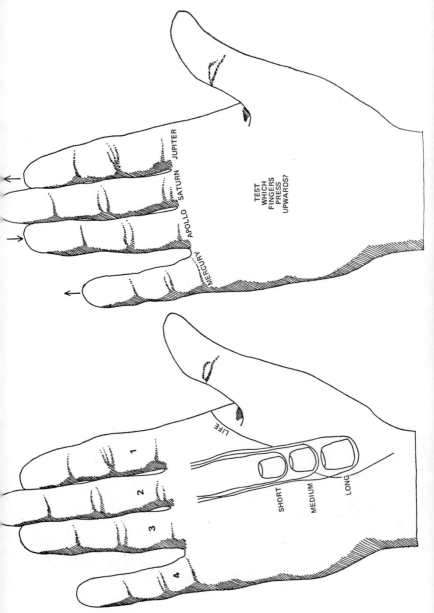

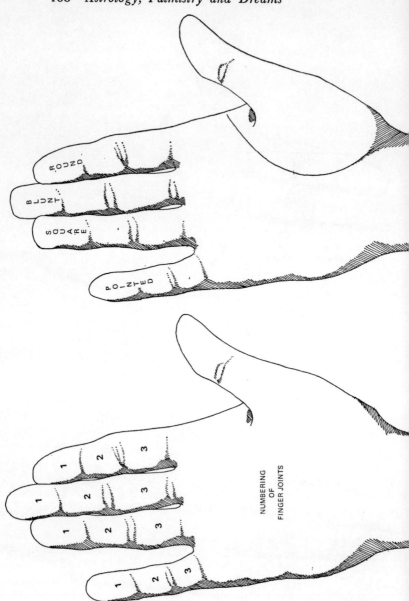

ROUND

BLUNT

SQUARE

POINTED

NUMBERING
OF
FINGER JOINTS

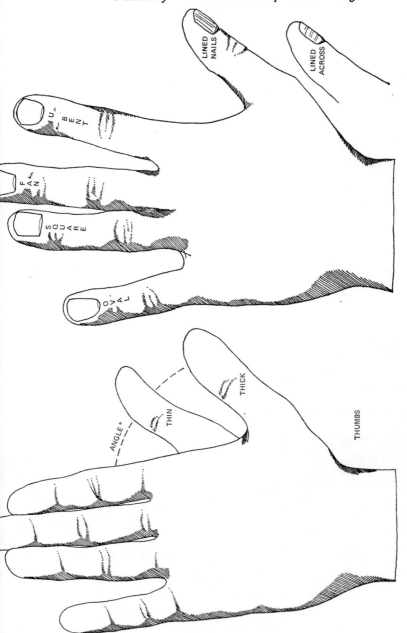

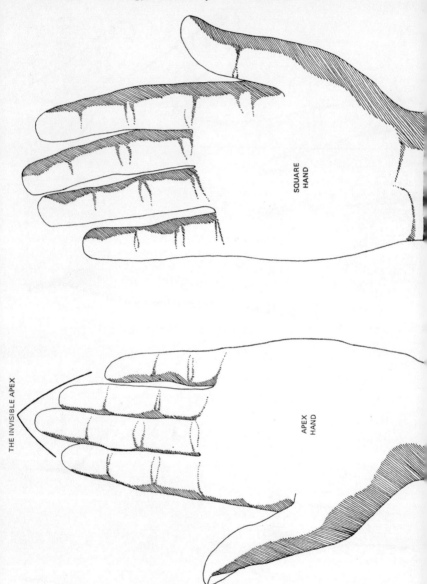

SQUARE
HAND

THE INVISIBLE APEX

APEX
HAND

FINGERS	LONG	SHORT	MEDIUM	SIGNIFICANCE
	ALL FINGERS			Systematic, orderly, practical.
Pointed	Long			Imaginative, idealistic.
Square	Long			Efficient and hardworking.
Blunt	Long			Lots of physical energy.
Rounded	Long			Artistic talents.
Pointed	ALL FINGERS	Short		Lazy, over-indulgent, poor worker.
Square		Short		Fits in easily with routine, does not work well alone.
Blunt		Short		Earthy type, likes all the physical joys of life, hard sports, etc.
Rounded		Short		Artistic talents for plastic arts, pottery, etc.
All shapes	ALL FINGERS		Medium	A well-balanced blend of the qualities known.
FINGER JOINTS				
First Joints				Measure of sensitivity in the subjects governed by the Mount at the base of the finger.
Second Joints				Measure of the method and order with which subjects governed by the Mount at the base of the finger are applied.
Third Joints				Measure of the power with which the subject governed by the Mount at the base of the finger can be put into practice.
FINGER NAILS				
OVAL	Long			Artistic but often shallow.
OVAL		Short		Fault-finding, critical, over-conscientious.
SQUARE	Long			Clean, orderly, smart dresser.
SQUARE		Short		Sarcastic.
FAN	Long			Sensitive, easily hurt.
FAN		Short		Retiring, shy.
U BENT	Long			Open, honest, reserved.
U BENT		Short		Timorous, shy.
LINED NAILS	(Lengthwise)			Bronchial conditions suspected.
(Horizontal)				Overworked, nervous strain.

THUMBS

Test the angle
Ask your subject to open the hand naturally, palm upper-most. Note the angle which the thumb makes when it drops away from the side of the hand. Close to the side of the hand indicates slyness. Introversion. Very wide open shows an expansive, showmanlike nature. Extroversion.

Thick and Thin.
Thick. – Stubborn, contented nature.
Thin. – Pliable, ready for logical changes.

Long and Short
Long thumbs denote an energetic, pushful nature.
Short thumbs show laissez-faire nature.

HANDS
The more square the hand the more practical the person is. The more the lines of the outer fingers lean in to make an invisible apex (as per illustration) the more mental and spiritual the person is. Experts make many more classifications, but these do not always agree exactly.

HOW TO TEACH YOURSELF TO READ PALMS
  (i) Use the enclosed blank hand outlines to fill in the lines in *very light pencil* so that you can erase them if wrong.
 (ii) Memorise the position of two or three features at a time. This section of the book is specially arranged to help you learn it easily.
(iii) Do the exercises once a night until you really know where all the points and lines are – you can never be too perfect.

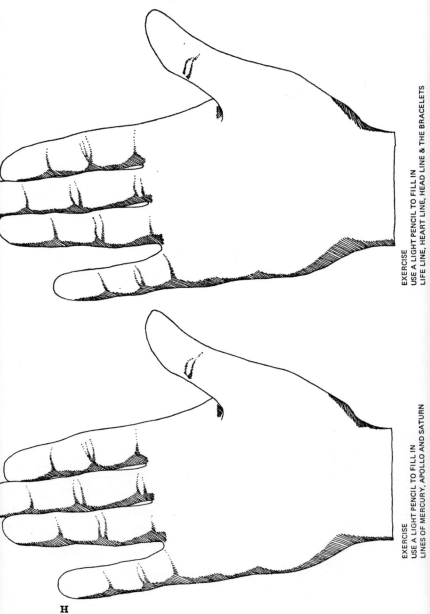

EXERCISE
USE A LIGHT PENCIL TO FILL IN
LIFE LINE, HEART LINE, HEAD LINE & THE BRACELETS

EXERCISE
USE A LIGHT PENCIL TO FILL IN
LINES OF MERCURY, APOLLO AND SATURN

H

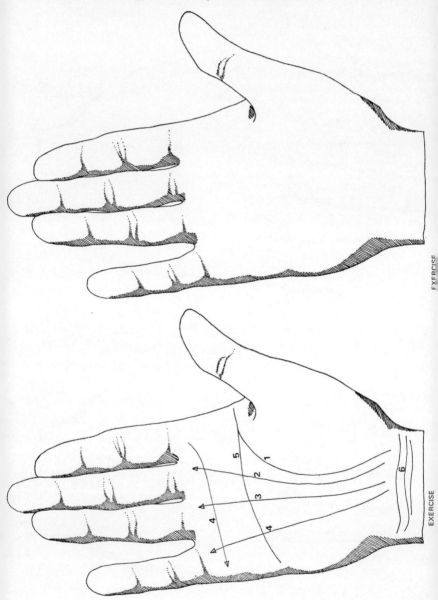

EXERCISE

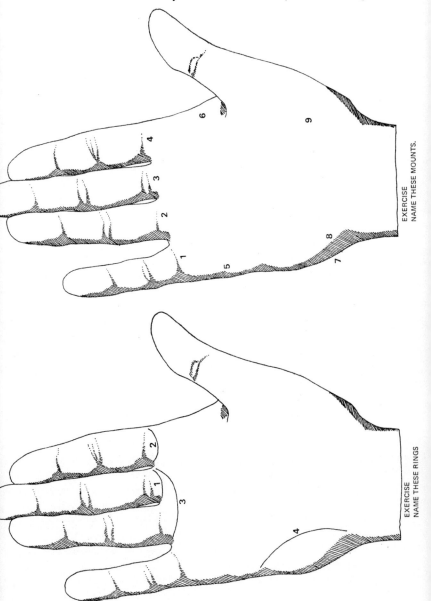

EXERCISE
NAME THESE MOUNTS.

EXERCISE
NAME THESE RINGS

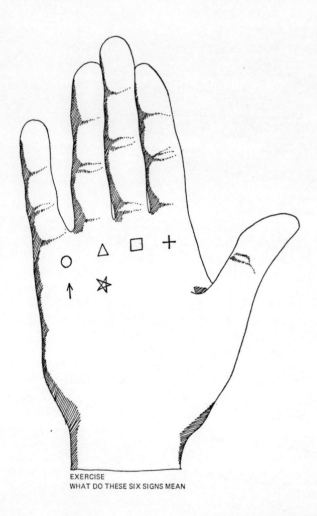

EXERCISE
WHAT DO THESE SIX SIGNS MEAN

Chapter 11

Dreams

Mme. Swetchine, the Russian authoress (1782–1857) who made her home in France, and wrote in French, achieved fame as a mystic. She wrote some thoughts which are poignant with meaning; among them :—

We expect everything and we are prepared for nothing.
But since the beginning of the Human Race Mankind has had dreams. Shakespeare wrote in the *Tempest* remarkable lines :—

We are such stuff as dreams are made of;
And our little life is rounded with a sleep.

There is a Chinese story of a philosopher who went to sleep and dreamed that he was a butterfly, and when he awoke he did not know whether he was a man who had dreamed he was a butterfly or a butterfly dreaming that he was a man!

There is seldom more startling proof that Man is not just a physical, material being than the process of dreaming. Hence Novalis, the unique poet philosopher, declared in his wisdom :—

We are near awakening when we dream that we dream.

The dream has been investigated by scientists who have tried to measure it with electronic instruments, strapped electrodes to the brain, and wondered where the music went to. My father and mother were both clairvoyant from an early age. My father lectured on spiritualism and spiritual healing; my mother could see auras, and by touching an object often tell many things about the owner although she had never seen him or her. Once I brought an antique Chinese teapot into the house. My mother saw it, touched it and had a fit of panic. ' Get it out of this house at once ' she insisted. The vibrations were bad. Much later I learned it had been a mute witness to terrible deeds of hatred and violence.

There are things in this world and in worlds adjacent about which we mortals understand too little.

There are things which no physical measuring apparatus can ever measure; the physical can measure only the physical. My own experiences would fill another book – or two!

This section of this volume is an attempt to suggest some interpretations (but not always exclusive) of dreams which are fairly common. One dream may show more than one symbol, and then it must be looked up part by part and interpreted accordingly. I am satisfied that many dreams which are true dreams (without any artificial means of stimulation, e.g. alcohol, heavy meat meals, etc.) are a form of spiritual guidance from the great world which is co-existential with the physical one we know.

Like the lamented Sir Oliver Lodge, the only physicist to explore the spiritual world seriously, I believe that in the ultimate case it is our physical world which is temporary and the spiritual world which is truly permanent and real.

Let us look at the atomic structure, ultimately the protons. Electrons and neutrons are nothing more than electric charges full of vibrations, the exact origin of which is unknown . . . and that is *solid matter* – a bundle of nothingness, tied together by magnetic forces in specific mathematically exact formulae!

The art of interpreting dreams is mentioned in the Bible when Joseph translated Pharaoh's dreams.

Allowing that there are wiser, more enlightened personalities than our own, acting under one vast Intelligence beyond description, we can readily allow that true dreams are to guide us and warn us, explain our mistakes and chances of success to us, but are carefully wrapped up in a symbolism which avoids our becoming frightened.

It is virtually impossible for the dreams we have to be bad. They warn us what will happen if we do not take avoiding action, confirm past history and guide the present, but do not usually predetermine the future.

Some prophetic dreams such as about the Krakatoa earthquake have been recorded in papers, magazines and later on authenticated. Prophetic dreams are also indicated in the Bible. If you see something terrible in a dream ascertain calmly, when you awaken, one or two things . . .

Firstly, that you are not suffering from indigestion, stomach pains or a fever . . . which conditions sometimes are neglected, and then brought in this way forcibly to your attention:

Secondly, that there was no specific warning, help or advice contained in the bad dreams.

If dreaming exhausts you, take a large heaped teaspoonful of honey in warm milk with a pinch of cinnamon every night before you go to bed; this will husband your strength. Some dreams recur, and as such are almost certainly spiritual messages, especially if three times recurring!

Of course much of the presentation is in the form of a dramatised incident, *which transcends all language barriers and fixes the events better in your mind.* If you doubt this recall Goethe's dictum, *Secrecy has many advantages, for if you tell a man outright something straightforward as to the purpose of an object, the man doubts whether anything so simple has any value.*

Dreams which come more often, or more than thrice, are not true dreams but a projection of a troubled conscience or a sick body.

Sometimes your advice will come connected with actual

recent events in your life, or connected to a memory of a previous existence.

When you are emotionally and spiritually very close to somebody a great deal of telepathy occurs through dreams.

Life here on Earth is a schooling. We cannot always see the teachers because their vibrations are at such a high rate that they are invisible to us for most of the time . . . just as an aeroplane propeller is solidly there but cannot be seen because of the speed with which it turns.

Teachers and loved ones want us to progress and learn how to live in a bigger world wherein we cannot make the same mistakes we make in this nursery world.

All dreams we remember have some spiritual meaning for us, linked in some way to some symbols we can work out and understand for ourselves.

Nor are all dreams solely linked to our mental progress and spiritual welfare. There is nothing wrong with profit (but much wrong with greed) so it is often intended that we should win money, progress financially etc. A friend of mine became quite well-to-do by winning races solely from horses whose names he dreamed about!

The attached list of interpretations are logical from the standpoint and arguments I have presented . . . but as Franze Werfel taught us in his book *Song of Bernadette* –

For he who believes no explanation is necessary,
For he who does not believe no explanation is possible.

DICTIONARY FOR DREAM INTERPRETATION

ABACUS : If you dream of this you are bothered with money problems, but care will help you solve them; be patient.

ABANDONMENT : You are frightened that one you love will leave you. Are you doing enough to keep their affection, or are you selfish?

ABBEY : You are nostalgic for the peace and quiet of the old religious ideas you had as a child (maybe in a previous life). You are overdoing it; slow down, relax more.

ABC: Should you dream of the alphabet in any way you are worried about your own (or a loved one's) education. Take advice how to achieve your aims.

ABDICATION: You are afraid of your own authority being lessened. Occasionally this might be prophetic for a political figure.

ABDUCTION: You fear stealthy misdeeds by another, or may have an unfulfilled desire for such deeds yourself. A problem is getting too much for you.

ABLUTIONS: You feel that something about you is unclean and have an overwhelming desire to get rid of it (maybe an unhappy memory).

ABOMINABLE SNOWMAN: You are dreaming of adventures, tired of your own mundane life. Try to break with your rhythms; get out and meet people, join new clubs, meet new friends. Travel more.

ABORTION: A sad dream indeed. Maybe it masks some terribly dismal event in your life, or the life of one dear to you. Maybe you are obsessed with the possibility of facing up to this. Seek professional counsel.

ABOVE THE WORLD: If you find your mind hovering far above your own body, above the world, but are able to see all the world, wish yourself back calmly, do not panic; this is a state which is very near departing this life, and you are letting unsolved worries and sorrows depress you too much. Seek spiritual guidance.

ABROAD: You are uneasy whether to travel, nostalgic after travel, longing for friends overseas, desiring to fulfil thwarted ambitions.

ABSENT FRIENDS: You have a guilty conscience about old friends. Do something before it is too late. Maybe a psychic warning.

ABORIGINES: If you dream of aborigines (natives of any kind) you have a hankering after a simpler life, especially one in which you can give vent to pent-up passions.

ABUNDANCE : Riches are coming your way.

ABYSS : You feel you are falling down a bottomless abyss – this means you are lacking in self-confidence; you must get help to build yourself up. Somewhere you are being too negative for your own good.

ACADEMIC HONOURS : You anticipate or long for success, and perhaps remember some glorious moment from a previous life. This dream may be to remind you of the potential for success that lies within you.

ACCELERATION : If you dream that everything is moving too fast for you it is because events in your life are getting out of hand; you need advice and help.

ACCEPTANCE IN MARRIAGE is usually wishful thinking, and anticipatory to a real, forthcoming event.

ACCIDENTS : To dream about an accident may be a warning, to drive more carefully for example. It may be a projection of a worry you have about which you are thinking negatively. Don't be so pessimistic; be careful.

ACCORDION : You dream of gay street music and musicians. Life is becoming too prosaic for you, give yourself a break.

ACCOUNTS : You are worried about money; maybe you are spending more than you earn. Sit down and think out all your expenditure, add it all up on paper. Writing any problem down in black and white is halfway to solving it.

ACCURACY : In your dream you are overwhelmed with worry about accuracy. Your work position is worrying you. Are you really in the right job?

ACCUSATIONS : You find yourself being accused of things which are false; injustice threatens you. Life is getting difficult, you need professional advice unless you can sit down (write your problems out on paper) and solve them yourself.

ACE OF HEARTS: Somebody is in love with you.

ACE OF DIAMONDS: Money is coming your way.

ACE OF CLUBS: Your luck will change for the better.

ACE OF SPADES: A lot more work is needed if you are to gain the success which will be yours.

ACID: Be careful, you may have offended somebody who hates you for what you have said or have done.

ACORNS: Good luck awaits you but you'll have to work for success.

ACRES OF LAND: Have you a suppressed desire to farm? Maybe you were a landowner in a previous life. Considered lucky.

ACROBATICS: Either you or somebody else performing. Projection of concern about struggle to succeed against terrible odds in life.

ACROPOLIS IN ATHENS: A distant memory from ancient days coming from an earlier incarnation.

ACTING: You are not being true to yourself, you are tired of the life you are being forced to lead. So change it.

ADDER: Somebody may be trying to betray you. Watch out for unexpected dangers, take more precautions.

ADDING UP: You are getting impatient with the slow pace at which life and success approach you. If you end on an uneven number this is supposed to be lucky. The number may be significant for you personally.

ADDRESSES: If you remember an address after a dream, go and investigate who lives there. Maybe you did yourself in a previous life. You might meet a person who will help your career, or one with whom you will fall in love.

ADJECTIVES: You felt inarticulate recently, and only now do words come to your mind. Learn your own language correctly. Take lessons.

ADMIRAL: You have aspirations or memories linked to this rank. Widely held to be lucky.

ADMIRATION: Secretly there may be a deep inferiority feeling within you. Take more care of your skin and diet, and others will admire you more.

ADMONITION: If you get a warning in a dream follow it up most carefully; friends in the spirit world are trying to help.

ADOPTED CHILD: Your life is incomplete, you need somebody else to help and love.

ADORATION: You have some unfulfilled religious and spiritual needs. Seek a spiritual counsellor.

ADORNMENT: You are feeling too lonely. It is your behaviour you need to *adorn* if you want more affection.

ADRIFT ON THE WAVES: No, no, life is not that bad, you are looking too pessimistically at problems, none of us is ever alone. Spiritual help is available, reach out to take it.

ADULTS: You are conscious of childishness in yourself, you long for good, stern, reliable counsel, and a shoulder to cry upon.

ADULTERY: Is this guilty conscience or powerful desire? This may be a warning to save you and others from much unhappiness.

ADVANCING TROOPS: You may be attacking another unnecessarily or they you – depending upon the direction of the soldiers.

ADVENTURES: It is time you snapped out of your routine and began to live a bit before you get too old.

ADVERSITIES: Your struggles will soon gain you success. Cheer up, and be more self-confident.

ADVERTISEMENTS: To connect yourself with a known advertisement means there is some emotional link between you and a person you connect to the advert. To dream of yourself advertising is awareness that you must push yourself more if people are to notice you.

ADZE: A quarrel can be avoided if you are wise.

AEROPLANES (AIRSHIPS): Either you are *flying too high* socially or financially, or else your wishes may not come true unless you work harder to achieve something.

AFFECTIONS: You are in need of more return for your love. Or you could give more love to one who loves you.

AFFLICTION: You are too afraid of illnesses, consult a work such as the *Concise Herbal Encyclopedia* and teach yourself more about what can be done to heal sickness.

AFFRONTED IN PUBLIC: Are you asking for it? Have you just been insulted? Be wary of others.

AFT ABOARD SHIP: You find yourself aft on a ship. You have a secret fear that life, love or age is leaving you behind – push yourself forward more. Care for yourself more systematically.

AFTERNOON TEA WITH A FAMOUS PERSON: You might succeed in meeting the admired person if only you made the best of yourself and of your opportunities.

AGATES: Somebody will help you, maybe with money.

AGEING: You dream you are getting old. Well, you are neglecting yourself. The older the fiddle the better the tune.

AGENT (SECRET): You feel danger around you, and you have to defeat it with sheer brilliant cunning.

AGONY COLUMN: Your name or another's is in the agony column of a paper or magazine. Somebody has failed you or you have failed another. Search your conscience.

AGREEMENTS: You are in urgent need of a contract, one is coming your way, be positive, do not doubt coming success.

AIR (CLOUDS): You feel the need of help and support in view of foreseen or real dangers and problems, but you are not seeking help from the right quarter, try again.

ALLIGATOR: This is the projection of a person who dislikes you and whom you instinctively distrust. Watch out.

ALLOTMENTS: If you dream of working on an allotment, you either are behind with such work or need an allotment to bring you peace and relaxation of mind.

ALMONDS: A symbol of fertility and of patience.

ALMIGHTY GOD: If you dream of God in any form it is a sign you are not as near to Him spiritually as you should be. Use your remaining years on earth to learn about the Eternal. Life here on earth is a schooling.

ALTAR: You have a wedding at the back of your mind, one past or one to come. Every marriage is what two people make of it, and in no way dependent upon what parents or others say. Make yours beautiful.

ALTERATIONS: In any form, clothing, buildings etc. Mean you have a deeprooted fear of changes, and are not adapting yourself. A Turkish friend of mine, Ahmet Mustafa, told me that Mahomet said *If you don't like times changing, change them.*

AMBER: Unknown wealth is yours, something you have is more valuable than you think.

AMBULANCE: There is help available if you do not leave things too late.

AMERICA: You may find more success abroad than at home. Have you thought of emigrating?

AMULET: If you dream of an amulet bringing you luck seek one out and wear it. The American Indians followed this totem system without fail.

AMAZON RIVER: Adventure calls you somewhere. You will never be happy until you do something brave and adventurous.

AMOURS: If you dream of love affairs you are cheating

yourself of the real thing. Why have an imitation when the real, genuine, worthwhile love is to be had for no more effort?

ANARCHISTS : If you have a dream in which you are among anarchists you are weary of the stupidity of the world, and in need of more spiritual enlightenment. If you yourself are an anarchist you are getting too impatient to solve any of your problems, seek advice.

ANCESTRY : You are failing your ancestral traditions. Discipline yourself better.

ANCHORS : To dream of an anchor or any anchoring reflects back to your position in life. Is it not time you settled down? If the dream is of an anchor being pulled up, you are too stick-in-the-mud.

ANGELS : This is to remind you that there are spiritual friends who seek to guide you to a happier and more successful way of life.

ANGLERS : An indication that you will get your desires if you show more patience.

ANIMALS : Perhaps this is a picture of a departed animal who loved you. If being attacked by animals see this as approaching danger from other human beings whose methods against you will resemble the behaviour of the wild animals you see.

ANVIL : (SMITHY) : Only more hard work will help you. Get down to it.

APOSTLES : You dream of one of the apostles; read up his life story, there is a hidden message for you in it.

APPARATUS (SCIENTIFIC) : You place too much reliance upon outside help. Develop your own abilities more.

APPAREL : You are wearing ragged clothes – you are too pessimistic, stop looking for the worst. New clothes – Good fortune is coming to you.

APPLAUSE FROM AN AUDIENCE : Try to live

more according to the dictates of your own conscience, not to be too reliant on the opinions of others, however much you love them.

AQUARIUM: You need more relaxation.

ARABIAN SANDS (Deserts): You are longing for the simple life.

ARCHERY (ARCHERS): You are striving to reach a distant goal. Work at it, you will.

ARCHES: You are passing under, or over. Experience is going to help you forward. In Tennyson's words: *All experience is an arch.*

ARENA (or BULLRING): You feel really up against difficulties. Courage, a cool head and resolution will help you out.

ARTIST: You dream you are an artist or are being painted by an artist. You may have frustrated ambitions to paint, to be painted, or may long to be the sort of person you would like to be, if so is dreaming enough? What practical steps are you taking to do it?

ATHLETICS: You dream of athletic performances, yourself as athlete or watching athletics. If you are an athlete this is a natural projection of your hopes for success, or fears of failure. Relax, realise that to try is the great thing, as Emerson's *Brahma* said :– *one to Me are shame and fame.* Try, trust yourself, and keep to the rules, it is better to lose with honour than win by cheating. This may be a spiritual warning to strive more to keep your body healthy.

AUCTIONEER (or AT AN AUCTION): Is money the only thing worth striving for? Are you devoting too much of your life for it? Think !

AUTUMN: *Season of mists and mellow fruitfulness* as the poet wrote. If you dream of autumn it may be a realisation that the autumn of your life is approaching, or indeed upon you. Do not be sad, this is to teach you that every season (and age of life) has its rewards, its beauty and its joys.

AVALANCHES: This may be inspired by some memory of a book, film or what you have actually seen; it shows a negative attitude to life, a conviction that you cannot win through. Try, try, try again! That is what life is all about.

BABYLON: Maybe an ancient memory of a past incarnation, or projection of a reader of history.

BAGPIPES: May indicate that you have unusual talent for playing this instrument, why not try it?

BAKING BREAD (OR CAKES): A spiritual indication that you will benefit by your connection with somebody who is talented in this sphere. It may be an encouragement to try more experiments in baking yourself.

BALES OF HAY: You are storing up luck for a future date, and soon it will come your turn to harvest it.

BALL GAMES: Your success and fortune are a matter of chance; you must exert more positive efforts.

BALLET DANCERS: You are not giving your mind enough time to relax, you need more exercise, and more beauty in your life. If you are a dancer it indicates that you are too concerned with your own performance, which will improve if you take planned time off to relax from it.

BALLOONS: (i) Blowing them up. Your hopes are high, make sure your efforts match them. (ii) Bursting. You must take more care in what you do or your aspirations will vanish into hot air.

BAMBOO GRASS: The toughest in the world. Difficulties await you, but slow perseverance will see you through.

BANGLES: You feel somebody is claiming your affections; if in the dream they are heavy the attentions are unwelcome; if the bangles seem light and pretty you are falling in love with that person.

BANKS: All dreams that include any aspect of banking are basically projective about your worries and needs

I

over money matters. You have two alternatives, either to examine your wants (how really necessary are they?) or to take advice on how to earn more.

BARBARIANS: You are beginning to realise how uneducated the mass of the world's population is; such knowledge is an initial step in enlightenment.

BARBER: You worry too much over trifles, try to be more hopeful.

BATHS: You dream you are swimming; there is a desire to be naked with somebody you love, to enjoy freedom to love.

BATTLES: May be a portent of some world cataclysm to come, or the projection of some sorrow within.

BAZAAR IN THE EAST: Your thoughts were of an oriental market. If you have no memories of such or no wish to visit one in the flesh, this could be a guide for you to try buying and selling whatever you remember being most conspicuously on sale there.

BEADS: See if you remember the number; that figure would probably be a lucky one for you during the coming week.

BEDROOM SCENES of any description only reflect various conflicts, fears and desires within your own love-life, occasionally a memory from another life with somebody who did not come back to earth with you.

BEER (PUBS, BARS etc.): A dissatisfaction with your social life is creeping in. Are you really getting as much out of your life as you put into the lives of others?

BEES: If just buzzing around you this betokens contentment and success; if they sting you this indicates a loss (pain).

BEGGAR: You as a beggar . . . you are ashamed to ask for help, but it would be given. Others begging from you . . . can you not give more easily?

BELLS: Good news on its way to you soon.

BENEDICTION: You dream you are being blessed . . . and so you will be.

BETTING: If you dream the name of a horse or a dog this is a good reason to back it as soon as you find it running. If you dream you are always betting this may indicate you trust your own ideas too exclusively.

BILLS: You worry too much. Try to remember that Rome was not built in a day, nor paid for in a month!

BIRDS: Your ambitions are escaping from you, try to bring them into reality by more effort.

BIRDS' NESTS: Money is due to come to you soon.

BISHOP: See *Abbey.*

BLACK CATS: Considered lucky symbol.

BLACK DOGS: Lucky symbol if they are friendly, unlucky if not.

BLIZZARD: You have got yourself into difficulties, ask for help; you cannot get out of this on your own.

BLOOD (Bleeding): Your health (or a loved one's) is in danger.

BLUEBIRDS: Spiritual uplift is coming your way.

BOATS: A yearning for travel may soon be fulfilled.

BOMBS: Turn away from the thoughts of anger and hatred which lie buried in the human soul; your spiritual progress is held back by unworthy thoughts.

BOOKS: Maybe you are studying too hard, damaging your eyesight. Or maybe you are being encouraged to learn more, the interpretation depends upon your circumstances. Maybe the answer to your burning problem is to be found in a book.

BOOTS: Only your own efforts will lead you to win, you are relying on others too much.

BOSS: Do not resent being led, if you do not discipline yourself to lead others responsibly do not blame another who is trying to do the job. You may have a guilt complex or deep hatred which you should try to analyse.

BRACELETS: See *Bangle.*

BREAD : See *Baker*.

BREASTS : See *Bedroom*.

BREATHE – UNABLE TO : You should get away from your present scene. You are liable to damage your health and finances if you do not move.

BRIAR ROSE BUSH : You are surrounded by petty jealousies. Beware.

BRIBERY : Are you letting yourself be corrupted? If not, beware somebody who may try to ruin your reputation.

BROOMS (AND BRUSHES) : You are being guided to make a new start in life, have courage, go ahead.

BROTHER(S) : You are neglecting your family or friends. If the brother you dream of has already passed on from this life to the spiritual life, think carefully whether he gave you any message which would help you or encourage you.

BRUSHING SHOES : You should give more time to small details in life.

BUBBLE BLOWING : Be careful how you spend your money, there is almost certainly waste somewhere in your expenditure.

BUGLE CALLS : Especially if you were in the Army, Navy, etc. The call, reveille, last post, taps, etc. are a warning to you . . . but only if you know what the call means.

BULL CHASING YOU : No, no, stop running away from your difficulties in life, turn round, you can fight them and win.

BURGLARY : This is a warning to take better care of your possessions.

BURIALS :—A warning that you have to make some changes in your life, maybe move home, maybe give up friends who are a bad influence on you.

BUTTERFLIES : Somebody you love is too fickle, and is betraying you, but are you causing this by your infidelity?

CABBAGES: You are too sedentary. Wake up and try harder.

CABIN, LOCKED IN A: You are being too careless, and likely to get into difficulties or danger unless you make more efforts.

CAKE BAKING: See *Baker*.

CALM SEA AND PLEASANT VOYAGE: An indication that you have peace and prosperity ahead.

CAMPING ALONE: Growing spiritual awareness and love of nature.

CAMPING WITH OTHERS: You are suffering from unrequited social instincts, or else projecting memories and desires.

CAMPING FOR SEX ADVENTURES: Your needs are unfulfilled. What are you doing to help yourself? Seek professional advice.

CANDLES: Light is coming to your mind. A candle being snuffed may betoken the death of a person who has helped you.

CARS: *Buying one* – this can be a spiritual guidance as to which make, year, price to expect.

Selling one – might be advice when and where to sell.

Driving one – an indication to be careful and not to relax your efforts until you arrive at what you want.

Crashing one – an urgent warning! Take one or two driving lessons to refresh your memory if you own a car. If not, keep away from cars and buses for a week.

CARDS, GAMES OF: You leave too much to chance, and do too little to help yourself practically.

CARPENTRY: If you are a *Do-It-Yourself* fan spiritual guides may be showing you new, exciting designs or techniques. Otherwise it is a general indication to help yourself more by your own efforts, not to lean on others.

CASTLES: Inside, wanting to get out: Open your life up, why are you imprisoning your Mind? Out, wanting to get in: Nothing is impossible to the virtuous man who tries hard. Be optimistic about your ambitions.

CAVES: (i) Exploring. You could be getting into wrong company; reflect what you are doing.

(ii) Trapped in one. Take time to think where your present way of life is going to lead you? Is it good enough? These interpretations would not apply if the dreamer were a caver (as sportsman) when this is advice to relax when out of the cave, and take more care when down one.

CHAINED UP: Is your marriage all it should be? Are you trying to build it up to be a thing of joy forever? It takes two to make a perfect marriage.

CHAMPAGNE FEAST: Some victory or achievement is to be won soon.

CHAPEL: See *Abbey*.

CHASTITY: This is a state of mind rather than of body, perhaps you are overvaluing the physical aspects of life.

CHATTING FRIENDS: Are you going to rule your life by other people's gossip? Do they pay your bills for you?

CHEESE: Probably a warning that your body needs more proteins.

CHEMIST: Your bodily mechanism needs urgent repairs.

CHERRY TREES IN BLOSSOM: Beauty is approaching your life, but be gentle with it or you will lose it.

CHESS: Your attitudes to friends and business are too serious, do not use human beings as pawns.

CHILDREN: You may have a repressed urge for a big family. It could be a phobia of a family.

CHILDREN PLAYING: You long for your own childhood, miss old friends, family, and feel insecure.

CHOIRS SINGING: Spiritual affection is being sent to you.

CHRISTMAS PARTIES: Anything to do with this

festival is a spiritual reminder of your obligations to keep old traditions. Always a happy sign.

CHURCH: See *Abbey*.

CIRCUSES: Excitement and fun will be yours soon. Expect an old friend to pop in to see you.

CLIMBING: Whether stairs, hills or mountains this is a projection of your deepest ambitions, need to get on in life, and according to the severity of the difficulties you dream yourself to be in so will you need to struggle to get on. If you are a climber, reflect whether this might be a psychic warning or guidance for you.

CLOTHES: See *Apparel*.

CLOUDS: You are not yet ready to receive what you want, you are creating difficulties for yourself which hold you back.

CLOWNING: Maybe a warning that you are giving people a false impression of yourself.

CLUB MEETINGS: See if you can remember what was said in your dream, because this could be a warning not to trust somebody too much.

CLUES: If you dream of being a detective this can be a psychic way of showing you to look for something important in real life.

COAL MINE: You need spiritual guidance to get up higher on a more advanced plane of thinking.

COATS AND HATS: An indication as to whether you are too protective or insufficiently protective to those you love – according to whether coats are being taken off, worn or put on.

COCK CROWING: Important news is coming your way; if it was a black cockerel expect sad news.

COFFINS AND FUNERALS: One part of your life is finishing, a new life is opening up. This is seldom an indication that somebody you love has died, the friends of the spiritual dimensions are too kind and tactful to hurt you this way.

COLDNESS AND ARCTIC SITUATIONS: Often a

sign that some extremely advanced spiritual entity has been to talk to you; such personages are usually accompanied by intense, unearthly cold waves, and you may well feel cold still when you wake up, even if you do not remember a message some help will have been given to you.

COLLEGE : See *Academy*.

COLOURS IN RAYS OR SHEETS : Without attachment to any specific objects to dream of colours may indicate changes in your own aura, or if around another person advice as to what their aura is.

WHITE : In the Western world – a wedding.

In the Asiatic lands – a funeral.

BLACK : You are despairing too much and not trying to reach up for true enlightenment.

YELLOW : Spiritual light is beginning to come through to you as never before.

ORANGE : A new burst of health and radiant life have come to you while you sleep.

RED : In any shade this indicates that there is too much passion which is indiscriminate, blocking your path to Awareness, Enlightenment and eventual Whole Enlightenment.

GREEN : Earthly prosperity, adventure and courage.

BLUE : Spiritual enlightenment and strong guidance.

BROWN : Too much concern for the material things of life.

GREY : Very primitive spiritual level.

Pastel shares are usually good, darker shades less so, i.e. lilac is more artistic and delicate than the pomp and ceremony implied by purple.

COMETS AND FALLING STARS : Sudden change of luck to be expected. If you are an astronomer this dream would be advice to look out for something strange and new in the sky.

CONCERT-GOING: Try to remember whether you liked the music or not. If you did, try to use music more to relax with; if not, get another hour's sleep every night.

CONQUESTS: Of any kind; if you dreamed you were conquered, think whether you are being used by others; if you are conqueror, reflect whether you are not unjustly exploiting somebody.

CONVICTS AND PRISONS: Either from this life or a previous life your conscience is pricking you, there is some wrong you should put right. If you can do a little kindness do it now, for you may not get another chance.

CONVENT: See *Abbey*.

CORKS POPPING: Expect to be invited to a party, somebody there may have good news or a happy message for you.

CORN: This is since the earliest recorded history of Man a profound fertility symbol; interpret it as such.

COTTAGE IN THE COUNTRY: Often a longing for a simple life, a weariness with the world's sorrows.

COURT CASE: Somebody will try to trick you.

CRIMES: See *Convicts*.

CROSS: A symbol of hope, resurrection and joy. Maybe you have a distinct call to help with some religious work. If a Moslim dreamed of the CRESCENT the result would be the same.

CRUTCHES: You are leaning on someone too heavily. Try to stand more on your own feet, help will be given if you try hard.

CUCKOO: A national disaster may be on the way, especially if it called in summer during your dream. Maybe one you love is unfaithful to you.

DAGGER ATTACK: Treacherous behaviour against you or by you, it depends who is holding the dagger. If you have gone against your own conscience see if you cannot make amends.

DAISY CHAINS: Or dancing among daisies, shows a yearning for purity.

DANCING IN PUBLIC: Soon people will acknowledge and accept the one you love, and more than ever before you will *be each other's own.*

DANGER THREATENS YOU: Take this as a warning, forewarned is forearmed, and if you take precautions you will avoid the real danger because of the dream warning.

DANGEROUS PLACES: You find yourself in a dangerous place. Then you are strong enough to get yourself out of it, but never scorn help from those you trust.

DARK NIGHTS, or PLACES: An indication that you are sitting in some degree of spiritual darkness. From the realms of Light friends are calling you to realise a higher destiny, showing you how helpless is the person whose mind is opposed by spiritual darkness.

DAWN (SUNRISE etc): A glorious symbol, it shows that great spiritual and material progress are coming your way now! If you dream that you had to wait for the dawn the figure of time you dreamed of was the number of days you must wait. Maybe on the exact day somebody quite ordinary will say some phrase to you, give you some idea which will enrich and change your entire life.

DEATH: Such a dream is not to frighten you, only to enable you to understand that the death of the body is not the end of us, only a change of form and a new beginning.

DEAF TO ALL WHO SPEAK TO YOU: Well, this is often an unpleasant dream, and its meaning is bad. You are not listening for spiritual advice on how to develop your life, and friends in the beyond cannot help you financially or with other problems either.

DEBT: You are in debt; well this can be interpreted as a moral obligation. Have you let anybody down lately? Somebody owes you something? Such a dream means that an outstanding reward will come to you.

DEFORMITIES OF THE BODY : In your dream being crippled is a sign that you need external help to 'straighten yourself out'. If you have the misfortune to be crippled, think carefully about your dream, in it there may have been advice which could lead to some miraculous cure, to lessen the pain, or help you achieve some success over your condition.

DELILAH : Your dream is a sign of betrayal of trust.

DEMONS (DEVILS) : You are seeking to personify the evil or absence of Goodness in men to explain away your own responsibilities for acts you have committed or think of committing.

DESERT LANDSCAPES : Your memories of this life or of one previous may have something to do with this. It may also symbolise your desperate need for sympathy and understanding. If you visualise yourself dying of thirst it means you feel your strength in combating the problems of life is ebbing away; get advice from a spiritual counsellor.

DESTRUCTION OF HOUSE OR A CITY : You are projecting your fears and beliefs into a dream; occasionally such dreams are prophetic, but mostly caused by unsolved worry.

DETECTIVE STORY : You dream of yourself involved in some great detective adventure. Friends from the spiritual world are beckoning you to explore clues as to why you are alive on earth, and what your mission is.

DIAPERS : You or somebody you love will soon become a parent.

DIAMONDS *are forever* as the song went; this is an age-old symbol that something beautiful will be yours for always.

DIGGING A HOLE : This could be a specific instruction to look for buried treasure, a lost personal memento, or else just a message that you have to sweat more before you are worthy of the success you long for.

DIRT ON YOUR PERSON : Ah, frequently this is a sign that you are repenting of some deed or acts done long ago, and like Lady Macbeth are saying : *Out damned spot!* Your conscience and friends beyond the veil are encouraging you to attain a nobler way of thinking and living.

DISAPPOINTMENTS : Often a warning to help you avoid the real thing.

DISCARDING CLOTHING : You feel you are not free enough to live the life you choose.

DISCIPLINE : You are being chastised . . . Your conscience is guilt-ridden. You are chastising another . . . whom you do not dare correct in public but should.

DISEASES : You should study to learn more about illness. If you dreamed of rheumatics, study my work *How to Defeat Rheumatism and Arthritis.* A dream about a special illness carries a special warning for you or a loved one.

DISGRACE : Somebody may use a weakness to discredit you. Beware !

DISGUISES : You may need subterfuge to obtain a goal, or maybe another is tricking you.

DISHEVELLED : You must bring more order and system into your life or only failure awaits you.

DISTANCES ON A VAST SCALE : Just an exercise to accustom you to the enormous size of the universe. Fear not !

DIVINITY : An explanation may be given to you in a dream of some of the spiritual mysteries. Think carefully of what you learned during the dream.

DIVORCE : A guide perhaps to your own relationships or of somebody close to you. A warning to avoid unhappiness.

DRESSING : See *Apparel.*

DRILL SERGEANT : An indication that you need more self-discipline.

DRINK (DRUNKENNESS): Your health is in danger. Drinking but never being satisfied – an indication that you are not getting anywhere in life; are you on the right lines? Try something else.

DUNCE: You see yourself wearing a dunce's cap. Shame at your own ignorance is overwhelming you. Put it right whatever the cost . . . education is your birthright.

DWARFS AND ELVES: You feel you are outstripping your companions or that others are holding you back . . . so why let them?

EAGLES SOARING: You are being called to higher achievements.

EARLDOM: A memory from some previous existence.

EARTH TREMORS: Possibly a warning; if you live in a quake zone move out fast.

EAST (MIDDLE-EAST): Historical or religious associations to have some special significance for you. Travel. (FAR EAST): Travel or historical memories.

EASTER: A symbol that you should hope and look forward to a new lease of good fortune.

EDGE (OR DANGEROUS RIDGE): Hold on, slow down, you are running into danger.

EELS SWIMMING: You have a long voyage ahead of you.

EGGS: A pleasant surprise is coming to you. If you drop or lose the eggs in your dream you will lose money.

ELEPHANT: In the East this is long held to be a sign of good fortune or of growth in wisdom.

ELOPING WITH ONE YOU LOVE: A flight from the real world; search around for more lasting solutions to your worries.

ELVES: See *Dwarfs*.

EMERALDS: Good fortune will come to you through buying and selling.

ENEMIES: If you have a clear conscience nobody can

ultimately harm you. *Nothing that is evil can permanently endure* said Carlyle. Tune yourself to higher thought as the best protection.

ENGAGEMENTS: Love is surrounding you. Have no fear. If you are honest, sincere and courageous all will come right in the end.

ENGINEERING: If your work is connected with this it may be a projection of your worries into your dream-life. Otherwise it is indicative of complications.

ENVELOPE, SEALED. YOU CANNOT OPEN IT: Such a dream is a sign that others are keeping secrets from you. Be less trusting.

ENVY: Others are jealous of your abilities or looks.

ESCAPE FROM PRISON OR ANY CONFINEMENT: You are lacking in self-confidence. You have let others drive you into some worrying position – only your courage and determination can save you.

EXAMINATIONS: If you are a student you may be worrying too much. Sometimes the dream contains a clue about one or two things which require revision.

EXECUTIONS: A change in your way of life and possibly in your place of residence. Do not be frightened; this is merely to draw your attention to things you can put right.

EXPLOSIVES: Beware an inclination to settle arguments by your emotional reactions. Think what effect your words (and deeds) can have on another.

EYES STARING AT YOU: Stop and think what you have been doing. Could you talk about it to God without any feelings of shame?

FACES LOOKING AT YOU: Same as for *Eyes staring*. If the face is of a departed friend or relative remember that there was almost certainly a message for you.

FAIRS: See *Circus*.

FAIRIES: See *Dwarfs*

FALLING FROM A GREAT HEIGHT: Without more effort your ambitions can crash to the ground.

FAMILY REUNIONS AND PARTIES: You are better loved than you think (even if you haven't got a family yourself).

FASHIONABLE CLOTHES OR PLACES: A deep-rooted need for smart things and travel, etc. Maybe you will get a lucky change of fortune or job, but you must make an effort yourself.

FATHER: A communication from him. Warning or advice. Even if your father is no longer in the world of the flesh you can still receive messages from him, provided you listen.

FEET: Watch where your habits are leading you.

FERRY ACROSS A RIVER: Try to remember how wide it was in your dream, or how long it took. Help will come to aid you like *a bridge over troubled waters*; the number concerned will tell you when.

FIGHTING: Boxing, wrestling, judo, fencing, with any method or and weapons. Symbolic of your combative spirit and determination to win through.

FIGURES IN DREAMS TELL YOU: Hours, days, months perhaps, how long you must wait for something you want.

FIRE: Maybe a prophetic warning. Otherwise a guidance that something is getting almost out of control in your life.

FIREWORKS: Somebody near you has a shallow nature.

FISH, SWIMMING: Adventure and travel beckon.

FISHING: Advice that you need relaxation more.

FLAGS: A prognosis of travel.

FLIES: Your health is in some danger, have a check up.

FLOWERS: Beauty and peace will be yours.

FLOODS: Much good fortune awaits you in later life.

FLYING: See *Eagles*.

FOG: Something is slowing you down in life.

FOOTBALL: The interpretation depends upon what you do in the match, obviously, scoring a goal indicates success coming to you. Watching it in a dream means you are getting too negative about things in general.

FORESTS: Peace of mind will be yours.

FOUNTAINS: You have much to learn.

FOXES: Somebody is trying to trick you. Honesty will defeat him or her.

FRIENDS: All of us have friends among the dead as well as among the living. Yours will help you greatly.

GAFF RIG: You have an urge to enjoy a sea journey.

GAGGED AND BOUND: You may have made or may make an unhappy marriage. Try to mend it.

GAMBLER: Have a week off to rethink your finances.

GHOSTS: Nothing to frighten you, just a lesson to remind you of life after death of the body.

GIANTS AND OGRES: My grandfather taught me that it is not the big ones who do all the work. Try to develop more self-confidence.

GIBLETS: Possibly advice on how to use them in cooking, many herbs such as tarragon can be used with them. If you were a cook or chef in a previous life this might be a link memory. Consult *Herbs for Cooking and Healing*.

GLADIATOR IN THE ARENA: See *Fighting*.

GLASS BREAKING: A person is more sensitive than you bargained for, somehow you have hurt them. Make amends quickly.

GOLD: Do not place so much reliance on money alone. Watch your health.

GRAIN: See *Corn*.

GRASS: A symbol of peace and forgiveness.

GRAVES: See *Burials*.

GUESTS: Advice that some are on their way to you.

GUNS: See *Fighting*.

GYMNASTICS: Socrates said *it is a shameful thing if a man (or woman) should grow old without knowing what grace and beauty the human body is capable of. Use your body better.*

HAIR (HIRSUTE): Growing hair means wealth, falling hairs mean you are getting careless about money and possessions.

HAMLET: Read through Shakespeare's play, there is some message which will help you there.

HANDS: Learn to value your own work more, you disparage yourself too much.

HANDKERCHIEFS: You are forgetting something.

HANDWRITING: You owe somebody a letter.

HARBOUR: Your ship will come home one day, fully laden.

HAREMS: See *Bedroom Scenes*.

HARVEST: Expect good fortune soon.

HATS: See *Coats*.

HATRED: This destroys he who hates more rapidly than the one who is hated is hurt. Try to clean it out of your mind.

HEATHER: Maybe Scottish memories from this life or earlier. Often a lucky sign . . . especially if the sun shone upon it in your dream.

HEDGEROWS: You must surmount your own faults before you can enter into the harvest of your own desires.

HELL: See *Demons*.

HEN AND CHICKS: Domestic bliss is growing around you.

HERBS: Your well-wishers are trying to direct your attention to safer forms of medicine. In some cases you may be receiving advice to become a herbalist yourself.

HERD: Whether of cattle, horses, reindeer, a sign of wealth waiting for you.

HEROISM: You are dreaming of being involved in acts of bravery and endurance. A sign that there are powers within you which you have either not tried out enough or not developed fully.

HIDING IN FRIGHT: You have a dream, often recur-

K

ring, that you are hiding. And true enough this is—from yourself; you are not facing facts squarely. Maybe an analyst will help you sort yourself out.

HILLS: See *Climbing* and *Edges*.

HOLES: See *Caves* and *Falling*.

HOME: If you are away from home it is a sign that you should write or visit it. If your home is no more, it is encouragement to build up some home modelled on the best aspects of your childhood home.

HONESTY: Somebody doubts yours, be careful.

HONEY: See *Bees*.

HOODED MONKS: People who pretend to wish you well are secretly jealous of you, be careful.

HOOTING CARS etc.:   You are moving too slowly for your own good. Examine your life, and try to advance.

HORSES: Projected wishes for freedom, to break loose from your surroundings. A sign of aspiration and desires which have not been realised. If you visualise a race and get the name of a winner, waste no time, seek out a race card and find out where and when the horse is running, it will invariably win. I have a friend who has made substantial gains this way, his dream-horses never lose. Usually it is for the day following the dream.

HOUSE: See *Home*.

HOROSCOPES: If your dream of a constellation, or planet, this will have an influence on you soon. Check up on the astrological section of this book.

HURRICANES: A feeling that you can no longer cope overwhelms you. Something in life is blowing you over. A change of direction in your thinking is advisable.

HYACINTHS: The ancient Greek legend tells of Hyacinthos who was killed by the savage jealousy of another (the flower sprang from his blood where he died). Do be careful of others' jealousy.

ICE: See *Coldness*.

IDOLS (STATUES):   You are placing too much reliance

on the opinions of others who are inwardly cold to you.

ILLNESSES: See *Diseases*.

INCENSE BURNING: Either in a temple or a church the meaning is clearly a memory either of this life or of one in your distant past. Try to recall more carefully whether the smell was beautiful or not; if not it is a warning from beyond that somebody is plotting something bad for you. If the smell is beautiful peace and prosperity are approaching you. Do nothing to deter them.

INFANCY: See *Children*.

INFERIORITY: A dream that conveys this is an encouragement to you to build yourself up.

INGRATITUDE: Such a dream conveys a warning.

INJURIES (HURTS): A warning that you are being careless. Such dreams are sent to help you avoid the real trouble.

INQUISITION: You dream you are being tortured for your beliefs and ideas. This is spiritual encouragement to hold on firmly; others have suffered much more in the past for the same reasons.

ISLANDS (Marooned): You are either not trusting others enough or you have been so hurt by somebody that you feel a need to recuperate alone. Don't stay alone too long. See *Hiding*.

JACK: Of diamonds. A friend is after you only for money.

Of Hearts: A friend desperately needs your love.

Of Clubs: Your luck is going to change.

Of Spades: You are not working hard enough to deserve the rewards you long for.

JACK TARS: A voyage or a trip by the sea is needed.

JADE ORNAMENTS: A long memory connected with Chinese, Maya or even Maori cultures; possibly you once possessed one.

JASMINE: See *Flowers*.

JEALOUSY: Clearly a warning either not to indulge in this yourself . . . you can *never* be happy with somebody who does not return your love, so look elsewhere. Or this is a warning that someone is jealous of you.

JEWELS: According to type. See *Diamonds* etc.

JOCKEYS (RACES): See *Horses*.

JOURNEYING: This depends on where you travel, how you go, etc. It may be advice that your circumstances will change. Try to recall every detail to facilitate further interpretation.

JUDGMENT: You find yourself in the dock being judged. You are letting others' opinions influence you too much. Assert yourself more.

JUNGLES (TARZAN ADVENTURES): The deep-rooted call of the wild is appealing to you. Give yourself a natural holiday as soon as possible. Try camping, caravanning, etc.

KANGAROOS (AUSTRALIA): You are trying to skip over essential things in life; take things more slowly, persevere, and you will get on better.

KEYS: Secrets long hidden from you will soon be explained.

KINGS AND QUEENS: Lucky sign. Quite often a distant memory from an earlier life when you may have been at court.

KNIFE: See *Dagger*.

LADS: See *Children*.

LADDER: Jacob dreamed of one leading to Heaven. This always denotes a chance for you to advance mentally, financially etc. See *Falling*, and *Edges*.

LAMPS (CANDLES, ELECTRIC LIGHT etc.): A symbol that soon spiritual enlightenment will make your life easier.

LAND (FARMS etc.): A hankering after a real home, desire to own something, and acceptance of need to work for it.

LARKS RISING: A new Spring will come to your life.

Joy which you no longer dare to hope for will come to you.

LAUGHING AT YOU: You have a most unhappy dream; others are mocking you. Do not place much value on the opinions of others.

LAVENDER: See *Flowers*.

LEAVES FALLING: You are wasting your life. Do something more positive and worthwhile.

LEGAL TROUBLES: A warning to you to avoid conflict with the law.

LETTERS: Act calmly when a letter comes, the news may not be so bad as you think at first.

LIGHTS: See Lamps.

LIONS: Read up Leo under the astrological section.

LOCKS: See *Keys*.

LOOMS (WEAVING): You need more patience and more regularity in your life.

LOSSES: Such a dream is to help you avoid losses, not a definite trend.

LOVE: See *Affections*.

LUGGAGE: Possibly some secret is locked away in a bag, trunk or case in an attic. Go through them carefully, the solution to an old problem is hidden away – find it. Possibly a journey is indicated.

MACHINES: See *Engineering*.

MADHOUSE: You dream of being in a madhouse. You must take some professional advice and perhaps spiritual guidance. Your health and your way of thinking are at fault.

MAGIC (CONJURORS): An encouragement to you to hope; there will appear an unexpected offer of help and solution to your difficulties from a source you do not expect.

MAPS: You should study more carefully where you are going in life. You really must plan your objectives more carefully or your talents will be wasted.

MARCHING. In an army: You must seek teamwork for

your happiness and success. In a procession: You must think more for yourself; others may help with words but will not pay your bill.

MARITIME ASSOCIATIONS: See *Jack Tars* or *Admiral, Boats*.

MARINE PARADE: At a seaside resort. You need a holiday.

MARKETS: You should be careful, some of your money is being wasted.

MARRIAGE (WEDDINGS): This dream in any form is guidance about your own marital status, somewhere in the dream was a lot of help for you.

MAZE (OR LABYRINTH): You feel that you have lost direction in life. You should seek spiritual guidance. Take yourself in hand; this is encouragement for you to make progress.

MEDICINE (HOSPITALS): Your health is in need of a check-up. Don't panic, you have been warned in time.

MILKING A COW: You are exploiting somebody unfairly.

MIME: You could do well to imitate a good example.

MIRACLES: A very spiritual indication that you are not alone in this world; help of a spectacular nature is coming to you.

MIRTH: Good if people are laughing with you, bad if laughing at you.

MISSIONARIES: Are you trying to teach another some truths? There may also be some ancient memory concealed here.

MIST: See *Fog*.

MONASTERY: See *Abbey*.

MONEY: Either you are giving it out or receiving it. So it is good or bad.

MORNINGS: See *Dawn*.

MORMONS: You may have a distant folk memory here. Take advice.

MOSES : Somewhere in the Book of Genesis is a message to guide you.

MOSS : Slowly you will accumulate worldly goods.

MOTHS : See *Butterflies.*

MOTHER : A memory of home, childhood. Maybe a communication for you, especially if the mother has passed on to the higher plane.

MOVING : Where you dwell at present is unfavourable for your welfare and development, look around to see if better possibilities present themselves.

MUSHROOMS : There are people who are living on your brains and your efforts, you are somehow being exploited. Watch out.

MURDER : Be careful not to arouse hatred or jealousy in others. Do not be afraid, forewarned is forearmed.

MUSIC (CONCERTS etc.) : See *Concert-going.*

MUSTANGS : See *Horses.*

MUTE : You cannot speak to somebody. In real life there is probably some terrible embarrassment, but when you make the effort to tell the truth you must say courage will come to you.

NAG : See *Horses.*

NAILS AND HAMMER : You will have to be more precise if you want to reach your goal; avoid being haphazard.

NAMES : If you hear strange names in a dream this can be one of two things : either somebody you are going to meet will be a good friend to you (unless the dream warns you against that person), or else a memory from your past.

NARROW MOUNTAIN PASSES : See *Edges* and *Falling.*

NAVIGATING DURING A GALE : A dream to show you that your ability to handle your affairs is better than you think, and show you what not to do in a crisis.

NECKLACES ON YOU: See *Adornment* and look under names of *Diamond, Emerald,* etc.

NEEDLES (PINS): If pointing to you somebody is being spiteful about you behind your back. If away from you towards another person, you are hurting somebody more than you think.

NESTING BIRDS: You will never be truly poor, some of the simple joys of home life will always be with you.

NETTLES: See *Herbs.*

NETS (OF FISHERMEN ETC.): You are in trouble, you feel you cannot get out. Ask for spiritual guidance.

NEWSPAPERS: You read of yourself or of a friend in a newspaper: some fame is coming to the person named.

NIGHT TIME: See *Dark Nights.*

NUMBERS: See *Figures.*

NUTS: You have a problem or a hold-up in what you want to do. But eventually you will solve the problem.

OAK TREES: Sacred to the ancient Druids, a tree which is fraught with mystery. You are going to experience some mystic wisdom which will affect your entire future for the good.

OARS: Yes, you really will have to put your hand to the oar; you are not making enough effort, and are in danger of drifting backwards, downstream.

OCEAN: See Seas.

OBELISKS: You have doubts about your sexual potency; take more care of your health.

OCCULT: If the dream frightens you what you have read or been told is wrong, your teachers have misinformed you, seek other guidance. If the dream pleases you, have no fear, you will learn more.

OFFICES: Your dream of work is unhealthy, you are attaching too much importance to this one facet of your life.

OIL WELLS: There is some trait of genius in you which has yet to emerge.

OLD PEOPLE: See *Ageing*.

OLDEN TIMES: Connects with memories of past lives.

ONIONS: Peeling them is a sign that somebody you place trust in has no depth; you remove one skin, then another, and another until you reach a hollow centre.

ONYX: You should wear something with a little onyx in it (it should have a yellowish streak) for the next year.

OPALS: A person you love is changeable, but do not despair.

OPERA – A VISIT TO THE: According to which opera you dreamed of so the story contains some example or story for you.

ORANGE: This was the golden apple from the Garden of the Hesperides; it betokens that somebody is planning to delay you or to beat you at something.

ORANGE BLOSSOM: Expect a wedding soon, you will be a guest. If you are engaged this dream portends that you should think more seriously about the responsibilities of marriage.

OXEN: See *Herd*.

PAINS: You have an unhappy dream of pain; see *Diseases*.

PAINTER (PAINTING A PICTURE): You will find it difficult to have everything in life just as you want it. Adapt yourself a little more to others.

> (PAINTING A HOUSE, BARN, etc.): Make the best of what you have got in life, do not be constantly hankering after something new.

PALM TREES AND TROPICAL ISLANDS: You must make a supreme effort to get out of your humdrum life; do something original, be yourself, find some new job, new hobby, new friends, etc.

PARACHUTE JUMPS: See *Falling*.

PARCELS: Do not let other people load all their burdens on to you.

PARKS (GARDENS etc.): You need more time to relax, to enjoy the beauties of this world which are your birthright.

PARTIES: Depending on the dream this might mean too few or too many; you should adapt your life accordingly.

PERILS: See *Danger*.

PHOTOGRAPHS: The person whose photograph you see in your dream would like you to think more often of them (whether they are in the flesh or not). If you see a photograph of an unknown, soon you will meet that person.

PIANO PLAYING: See *Concert-going*.

PIGS: See *Herd* and *Animals*.

PINE FORESTS: You need pure, fresh air urgently, your lungs may be too full of soot and dust. Pines have good vibrations.

PIRACY: Watch out that your hard work and savings are not lost to you by theft or deceit.

POACHING: Are you taking something that is not yours? It could be a symbol of a stolen love, by you – or another acting against you.

POLICEMEN (AND PRISONS): Several interpretations are available; if you have a free conscience, it may be that you need the protection of others, or that your life is trapping you into a routine of which you are not really part.

POISONS: Be careful, somebody may be spreading malicious gossip about you.

PRIESTS: See *Abbey*. Maybe you were a minister in a previous life. If you are a religious person in this life, you are letting doubts and the burden of work render your efforts less effective; try to get into retreat for a few days to regenerate your strength spiritually.

PYRAMIDS (Of Egypt): A link with the great, highly-advanced spiritual thinkers of Egypt. Reflect carefully for any words you heard spoken, or any unusual thing you saw during the dream, it will be a master key to unlock some mystery for you.

(Of Mexico): You are sacrificing yourself too much and must look after your own interest more.

QUARRELLING: This dream will guide you how to avoid the unhappiness which stems from quarrels.

QUEENS: See *Kings*.

QUICKSANDS: Your trust in somebody may be betrayed. Try to be gentle, forgiving and more appealing.

RACES: See *Horses*. If a race between humans this is a message from the Spiritual Dimension that you should trust yourself and try harder to win through your difficulties; you have a sporting chance!

RAFFLES: See *Gambler*.

RAGS: Unless you work more effectively poverty could await you. Perhaps another job would suit you better, and offer you a better chance.

RAIN FALLING: A sign of blessings descending around you. Do not be afraid of present conditions, help is coming. If there is a deluge in your dream remember that your actions in the dream are meant to teach you how to behave during a crisis and not repeat any mistakes in real life.

RAINBOW IN THE SKY: A message from a divine origin will come through to give you hope. Whatever your faith (even none) do some spiritual exercises to put yourself in a state of spiritual readiness to receive it. Iris (the rainbow goddess) was a messenger from Heaven.

RALLY (MOTOR, etc.): You need more amusement. If a rally driver, be careful to rest before your race.

RATS (MICE): Petty, scrambling, contemptible people are trying to undermine your position. Be careful.

REELS: See *Anglers*.

REFEREE: You are taking your sport interest too seriously. Use it for relaxation and enjoyment.

RELIGIOUS CEREMONIES: See *Abbey*.

RESTORATION OF THE KING: Perhaps you have a thought about Charles II, a memory or a symbolic connection.

REWARDS TO YOU: Your dream is of you getting a reward, this may be because you are not getting your just deserts.

RIBBONS: See *Adornment*.

RICE GROWING: Your luck will get better when the rice harvests next time; inquire when this will be, and do your best.

RIVERS (STREAMS): You feel you are drifting with the current of life, but the current is not too strong for you. If you will only try to use more energy and effort to steer your way you will cease to drift.

ROCKS: See *Climbing*. Do not let obstacles defeat you.

ROPES: See this as an invitation to climb up in life. If the ropes are entangled see *Nets*.

ROSES: A symbol of physical and spiritual love surrounding you.

RUBY: A symbol of love.

SACK: You dream you got the sack from work. Do not fear, such things can be the beginning of something better, it merely means you cannot get any more spiritual or financial progress in your present job. Keep yourself in tune with spiritual forces and guidance and help will come.

SAILORS: Sea journeys may be coming your way. Possibly you have been at sea. A message from overseas may come to help you. See *Jack Tars*.

SAILSHIPS: See *Boats* and *Navigating*.

SAPPHIRE: Sign of a spiritual blessing.

SHOWERS OF RAIN: You will meet with a lack of enthusiasm. Be brave.

SIGNING A DOCUMENT: Read all agreements carefully before signing.

SINKING SHIP: You will have to change course, your present plans could lead you to disaster.

SKY: See *Clouds*. If no clouds in the dream expect to proceed without hindrances.

SMUGGLERS: Spend more time considering the advantages of honesty; even a small slip might land you in trouble.

SOLDIERS: See *Fighting*.

SPARROWS: See *Birds*.

SPIDERS (AND WEBS): You will have to show a lot of patience.

SPINNING WHEEL: Your creative ability is to be tested. If you pass the test you will prosper.

SPIES: Are you seeking adventure too dangerously? Beware of enemies. See *Disguises*.

STAIRCASES: Ascending stairs is a good sign: Descending is a bad sign.

STATUE: See *Idols*.

STEEP SLOPES: See *Edges* and *Climbing*.

STILTS: You are not being fair to others; treat them more as equals.

STINGS: Do not let the words and deeds of ignorant people hurt you.

STONES: If thrown at you interpret as for *Stings*. If you are throwing stones, stop hurting others unnecessarily.

STORMS: You have the feeling that life is getting so tough that you can barely fight on. Help will come if you seek it.

STRING: See *Ropes*.

SUICIDE: Your present manner of living will lead to a disaster. Seek professional advice, preferably from a spiritual counsellor.

SUNRISE: See *Dawn*.

SWIMMING: Your struggle is keeping your head above water, and you will reach the shore; your dream advises you to keep going.

SWORDS: See *Fighting*.

TABLES: You will triumph over those who hate you. See Psalm 23.

TALISMANS: If your dream reveals that a certain sign is lucky for you, get one made or buy one and wear it for a year.

TAR ON YOUR CLOTHES OR BODY: Indicates that you cannot escape from ill-deeds until you make amends.

TEA DRINKING (PARTIES): Friends want you to be more sociable and more easily approachable.

TEACHING: Life here on earth is a schooling; try to look around and decide whether you are learning enough about yourself.

TEMPLES: See *Abbey*.

THEATRICALS: Deception surrounds you. Rise above it, reject the illusory for the realities of life.

THIRST: See *Desert landscape*. Your desire for righteousness is recognised, help will come.

THUNDER: See *Storm*.

TIGERS: Nobody is so big that he cannot fall. However big and important the men who oppose you, if you keep tuned to the Infinite you will win.

TORCH: See *Lamps*.

TORPEDOES: Somebody is trying to torpedo your hopes; be strong, keep the spiritual laws, adhere to the truth, and they will fail.

TRAINS (TRAVEL): A journey will be yours soon.

TREASURES: Do remember that spiritual possessions are also treasures; do not put all your faith and hopes on money.

TREES: Peace of mind will be yours.

TRUMPETS: It depends what music they played during your dream. Good news, bad news, a passing . . . *So he passed over. And all the trumpets sounded for him on the other side*.

TUNNEL – GOING THROUGH A DARK: Advice that you are in difficulties but you must persevere to get yourself out of them.

UMBRELLA: You are sheltering beneath the opinions

of another. You must develop your own personality more.

UNIFORMS: You are an individual, you have a personality all your own; whether you realise it or not you are following blindly the ideas of others without thinking out your own decisions.

VALLEY: You must seek to develop your personality, you have a lot of spiritual steps to climb, it is time you began.

VANS: See *Cars*.

VEILED PEOPLE in your dreams, the same as *Hooded*.

VICTORIES await you, work for them to enjoy the rewards.

VILLAGES: Same as *Cottage*, which see.

VIOLINS PLAYING: Relax more in the company of music. If you remember a tune, that tune carries some message for you.

VISITS indicate just that.

VOLCANIC ACTIVITY: If you live in a danger zone get out at once, this is probably a warning. Otherwise, violent quarrels seem likely unless you are more diplomatic.

VOYAGES: See *Journeys*.

WAGONS: See *Cars*.

WAITERS: Either you do too much for others or you let them do too much for you. Think carefully about this.

WALKING: You have to strive hard and be patient to attain your ambitions.

WALTZ TIME: See *Dancing in Public*.

WATER: Changes and purification approach you. See *Thirst*.

WAVES: See *Storms*.

WEDDING: Yes, but not necessarily for you.

WHALE: A delay for your plans – as for Jonah's.

WHIPPING: Is your conscience forcing you or another too hard?

WILLOW TREES: A sign that one near you is too weak to trust.

WINDMILLS: Somebody near you has no character, but shifts with each change of wind.

WITCHCRAFT: You tend to ascribe to others more mental potential than you yourself could develop.

WITCHES DANCING ROUND A FIRE: You feel that your enemies have defeated you; this is a dream which is frequently met with. But fear not, if you are spiritually enlightened. *He who laughs last laughs longest.* Many a triumph is premature.

WOMEN: See Bedroom scenes. Probably a man's projected fantasies. If a woman speaks in the dream try to remember the message.

WRINKLED OLD PEOPLE (OR SELF): Age of the body has nothing to do with the age of the mind. Keep healthy and fear no ageing processes of the body.

WRITING A LETTER: This brings you a message that is important if you can remember what was written or had to be written. Otherwise it is only a reminder to write somebody who is waiting for a letter from you.

YACHTING: See *Boats* and *Navigating*.

YOUNG AGAIN: The dream shows you as young again, what would you do with your time if you had it over again? The message is for you to *gather ye rosebuds while ye may.* Use this life as fully as you can to build your mind up.

YULE: See *Parties, Family Reunions* etc.

ZIG–ZAG PATHS: See *Maze*.

ZOO: You feel trapped, unable to express yourself properly; well it is a sign for you to break out, be strong and seek your own destiny with the aid of sound advice from unselfish people who can help you.